Antigone and Macbeth

Antigone and Macbeth

Adaptations for a War-Torn Time

by Richard Engling

Polarity Ensemble Theatre, NFP/Chicago

Copyright © 2006 by Richard Engling

All rights reserved.

No part of this book may be reproduced, stored in a retrieval system, or transmitted in any form, by any means, including mechanical, electronic, photocopying, recording or otherwise, without prior written permission of the publisher.

CAUTION: These plays are fully protected, in whole, in part, or in any form, under the Copyright Laws of the United States of America, the British Empire, including the Dominion of Canada, and all other countries of the Copyright Union, and are subject to royalty. All rights, including professional, amateur, motion picture, recitation, radio, television, and public reading are strictly reserved. All inquiries concerning such rights should be addressed to: Polarity Ensemble Theatre, 135 Asbury Avenue, Evanston, IL 60202 U.S.A.

Book design by Jacqueline Lalley
Cover design by Cathleen Ann
Author photo by Rebecca Uhle
www.PETheatre.com

ISBN 0-9776610-0-8

Printed in the United States of America

Dedication

I dedicate these plays to those prisoners who are unjustly held by our nation and to the innocent Iraqis and faithful American soldiers maimed and killed for a President's lie. I write in the hope that Americans will be reunited in the dedication to decency and justice for all.

–Richard Engling

Antigone and Macbeth

Adaptations for a War-Torn Time

Contents

Foreword xiii

Acknowledgements xix

Antigone 1

Glossary & Pronunciation Guide 51

Absolute Macbeth 55

Polarity Ensemble Theatre: The First Season
by Ann Keen 167

Thanks to Our Patrons 171

Antigone and Macbeth

Adaptations for a War-Torn Time

Foreword

My opportunity to adapt Antigone and to direct Macbeth came just as America was suffering through a desperate period of soul-sickness. We suffered the attacks of 9/11, and George W. Bush launched what the Secretary General of the United Nations declared was an illegal war on Iraq.

Meanwhile, Bush had put in place an administration of unprecedented arrogance and incompetence. On top of the economic disaster that was being prepared for our children and grandchildren was the psychic debt of the killing of many thousands of Iraqis in Bush's war. If justice reigned, Bush and his cronies would be facing jail time.

Ann Keen has been my collaborating director from the start of this process. Ann and I wanted the adaptation of *Antigone* to speak to today's world situation. She views the political landscape from a different slant than I. We agreed, however, that we wanted to bring out the inevitability of war when societies demonize one another and reserve righteousness for themselves. With every side certain that they are doing the work of God (or the gods) and that the other side is evil, there is no need to consider the enemy's point-of-view. We can dismiss the notion that others may have grievances that ought to be addressed. We can brush aside critics and get down to the business of war as the only solution to the unrepentant evil of the enemy.

In times of crisis, empathy for the enemy looks downright unpatriotic. And so we agree with our leaders, for instance, that suicide bombings are acts of cowardice. Cowardice is easy to dismiss. It's easy to agree that we ought to find all these murderous cowards and lock them up or kill them. If we were to imagine ourselves in their shoes, we might start to wonder why these people are willing to give up their lives. Yes, we abhor the violence. We find the murder of innocents despicable, but if we allowed ourselves a moment of empathy, we could no longer see the act as cowardice. We would have to ask ourselves, seriously, what could drive a person to do such a thing. However, empathy is a quick and early victim in the march toward war, all the way back to the battles among the city-states of ancient Greece.

Students of *Antigone* will notice the addition of a scene in which Creon and Antigone speak in private, which does not occur in the original. The difference between what is said in public and private is one of the themes the script explores. The tyrant must hide his true motivations and present a manufactured image to the public. However, the act of hiding his own motivations obscures for him the motivations of others—especially those he sees as enemies. This clouding of his vision becomes the flaw that brings his own downfall.

I have also taken license with the speeches of the chorus. The original speeches included many references that were illuminating at the time but mean nothing to our modern audience. I have replaced some of that with lines that tell the story of Antigone's ancestors and the family curse that had plagued three generations of the House of Laius.

Adaptations for a War-Torn Time

As for the language, when we began collaborating on the script, Ann and I wanted to keep the "classical feel" of the play, so I have used a heightened language with rhythms and sounds that will work well for the actors. I strove to make the script readily accessible but still not totally modern.

What occurred to me about *Macbeth* in this war-torn time was that a production could be performed as a ritual for dispelling evil from the nation. *Macbeth* is, at its heart, a morality play. Temptation presents itself. Evil incarnates in the heart of Macbeth and his Lady. It culminates in murder. Murder leads to more murder, followed by retribution and damnation.

As the play begins, the Scottish kingdom is engaged in civil war. Forces loyal to King Duncan, led by Macbeth and Banquo, defeat the rebels. The kingdom anticipates a return to peace and justice. Instead, the hero Macbeth, encouraged by the witches, kills the king and usurps the crown. He rules as a tyrant over the realm. To hold on to his throne, he murders opponents and innocents alike, until the rightful heir to the throne can mount a force to defeat him. Finally, the tyrant Macbeth is purged and the kingdom can return to a time of peace and justice.

I envisioned a production in which Macbeth would stand in for the tyranny in our own society. Like the ancient ritual of the scapegoat, in which all the sins of the tribe are put upon the sacrificial goat, the sins of the American tyranny would be put on the performance of the character Macbeth. With the purging of the tyrant in the play, we symbolically ask our tyranny be purged, as well.

It should be noted that George Bush, for all his faults, was not the principal target of our ritual. As time goes on, Bush often appears to be more a pathological incompetent than a deliberate tyrant. There is a deeper tyranny that corrupts both Republicans and Democrats: the corporate dollar that debases our democratic process. Corporate money helps elect candidates more friendly to corporate needs than to the people, and corporate control of the media hides what is happening.

To play *Macbeth* as a purgative ritual requires very little change to Shakespeare's original script. The witches play a much larger role. They have additional lines and action at the top of the play. In the first scene, they "cast the circle" of the ritual in which the action of the play takes place. Macbeth is ceremonially carried onto the stage by masked pallbearers. With new lines added to Shakespeare's script, the witches invoke the spirits, asking that his destruction take along with it the corruption in our society.

> FIRST WITCH
> The circle cast: the magic's set,
> To cast a man forth for destruction.

> SECOND WITCH
> To take with him all our corruption,
> That surrounds this weal invisibly.

> THIRD WITCH
> Make seen in him; the gods to feed:
> Take him for us, that's what we plead.

The witches act as ritual priestesses in this adaptation. During the course of the play, they often show up as minor characters, carrying masks that disguise their identities to the other characters. They also carry ceremonial bird's wing fans, as are used in many Native American rituals. The witches use the fans to direct incense smoke, to cast away or draw in spirits and to make themselves invisible.

Audiences sometimes get the impression that the witches cause Macbeth's downfall by their deceptions. This is not

Adaptations for a War-Torn Time

the case. They act as catalysts to help bring out Macbeth's evil so that it can be purged. Macbeth had been giving serious thought to murdering King Duncan before he met the witches.

Note this exchange:

> THIRD WITCH
> All hail Macbeth, that shalt be king hereafter.

> BANQUO
> (to Macbeth)
> Good sir, why do you start, and seem to fear
> Things that do sound so fair?

Macbeth reacts in fear to being greeted as the one who will become king. He does so because murdering the king is already on his mind. Later, in an aside, he reflects upon it.

> MACBETH
> [Aside.]
> My thought, whose murder yet is but fantastical,
> Shakes so my single state of man,
> That function is smother'd in surmise,
> And nothing is, but what is not.

Despite the fear that shakes him, Macbeth carries out the murder, encouraged by the deceptions of the witches and the prompting of Lady Macbeth.

When he is finally defeated and killed by Macduff, the witches have their second additional scene. They gather around his fallen body and recite the invocation:

> WITCHES
> Now 'tis now, the tyrant's dead;
> Now 'tis now, shall lose his head.
> Thus we ask please free this world;

> From in our midst his evil hurl.
> And all around, this cure shall spread;
> Remove from us that which we dread.

The same pallbearers who carried him on in the first scene carry Macbeth off as the company sings a dirge to Kali, the goddess of destruction. The intention is that the malevolence in our society, like the malevolence in Macbeth, be destroyed, allowing the society to be cured.

To perform the play like this takes modern secular theatre back to its sacred roots. Early performance (and performance in many indigenous societies today) enacted stories in order to honor the gods and sacred spirits and to petition them for desired results. For instance, successful hunts would be acted out in order to pray that the spirits would allow animals to be captured and killed for the good of the tribe.

This notion might seem quaint in contemporary Chicago where we produced *Absolute Macbeth*, but science has studied the effectiveness of prayer. Experiments have proven that hospital patients for whom prayers are offered do better than those for whom they are not.

The question remains then: Is our society better off for us having done the play? I don't know. However, I did see the ritual have a profound effect on the actors performing the play and on the audiences who watched it. In the world of the theatre, that is enough.

Adaptations for a War-Torn Time

Acknowledgements

My thanks to Ann Keen and Zack Brenner for bringing the first professional production of *Antigone* to life. And thanks to Fredi Conley and J.D. Gonzales who directed high school productions of the script even before its professional debut.

Thanks especially to my wife Gail and my daughter Zoë Olivia.

Also thanks to Kathy Logelin, Bill Bannon, Elizabeth Kline, Drew Vidal, Kristy Kambanis, Rich Helland, Mary Mechler, Thad Anzur, Alexandra Helland, Charley Jordan, and Bobby Zaman who appeared in the first staged reading. And to Catherine MacCoun, Martin Uthe, David Yondorf, Jason LeCompte, Steven Marzolf, Abigail Trabue, Mason Hill, Dean Matthews and Lois Hobart for subsequent help.

Thanks to Jackie Lalley, Irv Gorman, and Cathleen Ann for designing and producing this book. Thanks to all the generous Polarity Ensemble Theatre Founding Patrons, who are listed in the back pages.

Thanks to Bob Fiddler, Gary Konigsfeld, Charley Custer,

Antigone & Macbeth

Ron Bognore, Carol Galginaitis, Bill Burton, Kate Bertrand, Catherine MacCoun, Bridget Sullivan, Al Gabor, Chris Patrakos, Jackie Lalley, Irv Gorman, Elizabeth Crane, Jennifer Roche, Steve Meiss, Janice Finney, Lynn Sloan, Maureen Holmberg, Ignacio Lopez, Megan Vaughn, Sharon Solwitz, Liz Davidson and others who passed through the Chicago Writers Group, and to Robert Bly and the teachers and men of the Minnesota Men's Conference for years of inspiration.

—Richard Engling

Antigone

Adapted from Sophocles' tragedy
by Richard Engling

Antigone & Macbeth

The world premiere of Richard Engling's adaptation of *Antigone* was presented by Polarity Ensemble Theatre at the Breadline Center for the Performing Arts, 1802 West Berenice, Chicago. It opened February 17, 2006.

Cast, in order of appearance

Chorus Leader	Erin Lane
Chorus	Robert Ertel
	Marsha Harman
	Laura Rauh
	Meaghan D. Sullivan
Chorus/Guard	Brian Bush
Chorus/Messenger	Travis Gauchay
Antigone	Abigail Trabue
Ismene	Amanda Monfrooe
Creon	Christopher Marcum
Eurydice	Abby Rowold
Haemon	Andrew Yearick
Teiresias	Richard Engling
A Boy	Joseph M. Ciresi
Understudy	Marc Rita

Staff

Directors	Ann Keen and Zack Brenner
Stage Manager	Mary Ellen Rieck
Fight Choreographer	Mason Hill
Costume and Mask Designers	Jessica Pribble
	Vanessa King
Lighting Designer	Tony Ligeza
Properties Designer	Wendy Mingin
Set Designer	Marissa Hughes
Graphic Designer	Cathleen Ann

Please visit www.PETheatre.com for information on a DVD documenting this production.

Antigone

SETTING: An open space before the royal palace at Thebes.

MUSIC. The CHORUS enacts in dumb show the battle for Thebes and the fall of the two brothers, Eteocles and Polyneices. Eteocles is carried away with full honors. Polyneices is left behind on the battlefield.

CREON
(from forestage, or voice-over)
Therefore, Eteocles, who perished fighting for our city in all renown of arms, shall be entombed and honored with every rite. But for his twin, Polyneices, who conspired with our enemies, let no one grace him with funeral rites, on pain of death.

(Daybreak, the next morning. ANTIGONE calls ISMENE forth from the palace, in order to speak to her alone.)

ANTIGONE
Ismene! Ismene! Come, dear Ismene, my blood sister. Let me see your face. Do you not feel the weight of the troubles Zeus brings? It is as though our father never left us. The gods refuse to forget his sin. They send more dishonor. Have you heard the edict?

ISMENE
If my face shows nothing, the exhaustion of grief has wiped it clean. I can no longer see what lies before me, but only our brothers driving their spears through one another's hearts. The city rejoices over the enemy's defeat, but I can think only of that final, bloody embrace.

ANTIGONE
And yet there is more. I must speak with you in private.

ISMENE
What new grief could matter after this?

ANTIGONE

I, too, felt empty and hopeless after our brothers' deaths. To kill one another over the throne of Thebes! But now that Uncle Creon rules, he sets himself above the gods! He allows Eteocles to be buried with proper ceremony. His spirit can join the honored dead. But hapless Polyneices lies rotting. His dead eyes shall be plucked by crows. Dogs will tear and rip his flesh. His intestines make a feast for vultures. And because of this, his spirit will wander the land, never able to join the ancestors. Good Creon forbids anyone give Hades his due. Can we, born of a most noble family, allow our brother to rot on the ground?

ISMENE

What would you have us do?

ANTIGONE

We must bury him.

ISMENE

If anyone were to see us burying Polyneices, we would be put to death.

ANTIGONE

You would rather allow uncle to play politics with what we owe the gods?

ISMENE

What we owe the gods would now be the most political act in Thebes.

ANTIGONE

My brother will not lie on the ground to be dragged by dogs. If you will not assist me, I will go alone.

ISMENE

Antigone, wait. I am too heartbroken and terrified to think clearly. How can we be sure what is right? Must we walk straight into our deaths? Have you no fear of dying?

ANTIGONE
Creon cannot interfere with the ceremonies of the dead.

ISMENE
You are just like father, always so certain. But think how he died, hated and disgraced. He would not rest until he discovered his own patricide and incest! Then the truth was so painful he tore out his eyes. Mother slipped a noose around her neck to choke out her shame. And now our brothers slaughter themselves, they who slept in one another's arms as babes. We two are all that is left: two solitary women against the royal power. Must we add our deaths to those who died before us? Can we not honor our own womanhood and cast aside the family curse? Let us obey Creon's edict and live. To do otherwise is to conspire with the most horrible of fates. Or do you believe this is what we owe the gods? Must every one of us destroy ourselves?

ANTIGONE
The very thing that holds you back, urges me on. Why should we cling to this accursed life? We are here for a few breaths, and then death collects us. How could you stand the shame if you arrived at Hades' realm and Polyneices were not there! Should we linger here a few more miserable years and then feel his loss for eternity?

ISMENE
I want to do justice for Polyneices. I want to mourn over both our brothers' graves! But if they discover us, we will not be allowed our quiet prayers. They will uncover his body, and we will die for nothing!

ANTIGONE
You must choose: Either oppose injustice or accept it. If we do not act against this abomination, we endorse it. Even if we fail, what we attempt means something. I cannot answer for you, but I will go to heap earth on my brother.

ISMENE
Misery has been our companion for so long. Now you embrace it like a lover.

ANTIGONE
Stay behind then, sister. What I embrace is my obligation to family and the gods. My duty is clear.

ISMENE
At least take care. Tell no one. I will keep your secret.

ANTIGONE
I will not sneak like a thief. Go shout my deeds. Silence in the face of depravity is hateful to me, and you will be hateful too if you cower before tyranny.

ISMENE
Your passion makes you reckless. I fear for you, Antigone.

ANTIGONE
Fear for Creon. It is he who thwarts the will of the gods.

ISMENE
But what if the only result of this is that Polyneices and you both lay unburied? Will you be satisfied to have both your spirits wander? I cannot allow that. You are more dear to me than anyone else.

ANTIGONE
I will do what I must. I know what offends the gods! I would rather die today than live a coward's life and suffer for eternity.
 (ANTIGONE exits.)

ISMENE
I want to go with you, Antigone. How right it would feel to bury our brother! But if you are put to death, I must see to your funeral rites—even if that should mean my own death. For now, I must bear the disgrace in your eyes. It

is my duty to watch over you.
   (Exit ISMENE as CHORUS enters.)

CHORUS

Sun-blaze, fair light that awakens Thebes,
You shine at last, eye of golden day.
Your dazzling light embraces us.
Your searing eye shames our foes home.
They came against us with proud white shields,
Roused by the vengeance of traitor Polyneices.
Like shrill-screaming eagles they swooped
Into our land in snow-white pinion sheathed,
With arméd throng, and helms feathered high.

They circled all around our dwellings.
They ravened round our seven gates.
Their spears thirsted for Theban blood.
But we drove the invaders away!
So fierce was the battle raised against them,
The very tumult turned many on their heels,
Our force too mighty for them to conquer.
Our heroes too strong to meet defeat:
The blood of our ancestors raged within us,
They who were born from the teeth of dragons.

LEADER

To share our throne were the twin sons of Oedipus,
Equal in birth, each to rule a year by turn.
But wise Eteocles saw danger to the realm.
Oft-changing rule would make us weak.
He refused his brother when came his time.
Proud Polyneices gathered our foes.
But Zeus hates the boasts of a traitorous tongue.
He beheld them coming in clanging gold.
With brandished fire he struck them down
As they climbed heavy armed upon our walls.

CHORUS

They fell to earth, torches in hand,
Their frenzy stopped, fear choked their throats.

Almighty Zeus wreaked havoc upon them,
An ally in our need, their army put to rout.

LEADER

And so seven captains came to seven gates.
They offered single battle to decide the day.
Seven Theban heroes ran with sharpened steel.
Each dared death to conquer our foes.
They took their rivals' swords to the temples of our gods.
But wait! What is this? Two men stand still.
Twin brothers, twin kings, with twin spears and twin hate.
They face one another with murder in their hands.
Each the equal in birth and strength.
The champion each of rival, vengeful gods.
Each drives the spear through his brother's heart.

CHORUS

So fall the heirs to the throne of Thebes.
But put this sorrow behind us now,
Victory brings its glory to all.
Let joy forget the gore and blood,
The hated enemy upon our walls.
Dance us now in the glory of gods
With song and drum throughout the night.
Let Dionysos lead our way
With holy madness ecstasy,
His wild dancing shakes the land.

LEADER

But hear ye now, the new king comes,
Creon, uncle of the twin-killed sons.
Our ruler takes power through the twists of fate.
    (Enter CREON and EURYDICE.)

CREON

Speaker of Thebes, distinguished justices, honored guests: This ship of state, wracked by the recent waves of terror, has once more come safe to harbor aided by the friendly winds of the gods. I have called ye, out of all

Thebans, because I remembered how true and constant was your reverence for the royal hand of Laius. You upheld his son Oedipus when he ruled our land, and when he perished, your loyalty continued with his sons. Now they have fallen, brother by brother murderously slain, and I ascend the throne with all its powers, by nearness of kinship to the dead.

(CREON turns to EURYDICE.)

We have lost many loved ones. No family has felt the harshness of fate more than our own. We lost not only our nephews, but Megareus, the elder son of your king and Queen Eurydice. Megareus, who would have been our heir to the throne of Thebes. Having heard the prophesy of Teiresias that a voluntary death would save our city, noble Megareus fell upon his sword in self-sacrifice. He died even before the battle began. My beloved eldest, nearest to my heart. Who can say that his act did not save us all?

(EURYDICE exits.)

The losses that we have borne bow us to the Earth. We must mourn, and we must give each other strength. No man knows himself until he be tested by both sorrow and power. But as Zeus is my witness, wherever the source of lawlessness, we will root it out, even if the source be our closest comrade. Our enemies embrace death as a cause and a creed. Only when our city stands protected can we prosper together.

We will honor the virtuous and condemn those who threaten our peace. Therefore, Eteocles shall be graced with the rites that follow the noblest dead to their rest. But for Polyneices, who sought to spill his kindred's blood and to drive the survivors into slavery, I proclaim to our people, on pain of death, that his body remain on the field of battle. He shall be left unburied, a corpse for birds and dogs to eat, a shameful sight upon the land. By this will our enemies learn the meaning of Theban justice.

LEADER
Creon, King, we have heard your edict. Your word is law.

CREON
See then you execute what I ordain.

LEADER
Good king, this charge is better laid upon your men at arms.

CREON
Fear not, I have posted guards to watch the corpse.

LEADER
What duty, then, would you put on us?

CREON
That you do not side with those who break my law.

LEADER
Do you believe us mad enough to court our own deaths?

CREON
Bribery and ambition often lure men to ruin.
   (A GUARD enters.)

GUARD
My lord, I will not pretend to pant and puff like some swift-footed messenger, for often did my thoughts make me pause, and wheel round in my path. The debate stormed in my mind: "Why hurry headlong to your fate, poor fool?" But on the other hand: "If Creon learn this from another, you will rue the day!" And yet again: "What am I to tell him?" For mystery indeed hangs over this happenstance. Thus with jerks and starts I hastened slowly on my road, with many tumbling thoughts extending a yard to a mile. But the advance voice won out, that I should come before you. Though my tale may bring me to disaster, yet will I tell it; for I come knowing I can suf-

fer nothing that is not my fate. For if it is my fate to suffer, then suffer I shall regardless.

CREON

Speak, please. What is your news?

GUARD

May I premise with one word more about myself? It is true that I have not solved the mystery—but then neither did I do the deed nor see it done, and therefore it would not be just that I should come to harm for the mere reporting of it.

CREON

Shall we dance until the morrow, or will you speak your message?

GUARD

The bearer of dread tidings must often quake. I beseech of you, skewer not the messenger.

CREON

Then, fool, tell your news and get you gone.

GUARD

My liege...the corpse of Polyneices is buried. Someone has besprinkled it with dust and performed other such rites as piety enjoins, and has gone.

CREON

Who dared do this thing?

GUARD

I know not, though we searched a half league around. There was no trace of pick or shovel. The ground was hard and unbroken—not a scratch or rut of chariot wheels—nor sign of human hands at work. When the first sentry of the morning watch gave alarm, we all stood terror-struck. The corpse was vanished! But on second look, it was not gone, nor interred in earth, but covered over with just enough soil so as to avert the curse that haunts the unburied dead. Of vulture or jackal there was no sign. Recovered from the first shock, we investigated with a diligent thoroughness, but finding not a clue, we began to dispute. Guard railed against guard and bared fists. Each in turn we suspected of the deed, but each in turn offered his alibi. We challenged one another to handle red-hot iron, or pass through fire, affirming thus our oaths of innocence. We argued until one voice spoke the words that bowed us to the ground like quivering reeds: "King Creon must be told." After much silence, we cast the lots, and I drew the short straw: to be the bearer of bad news that no man welcomes.

LEADER
I must confess, I had misgivings from the first, my liege. Can this deed possibly be the direct work of gods?

CREON
Have you no more wit than this guard? The gods do not cherish this traitor. He came to set fire to their temples! We must vanquish those who conspire towards lawlessness. A sack of gold is more powerful than a thousand swords when it causes steady men to retreat their oaths. Clearly, my enemies corrupt my guards with bribes. Evil has power, and it must be opposed.
   (to GUARD)
Hear me now: as I revere Zeus, by Zeus I swear, except that you find and bring me the man who carried out this lawless burial, death shall not suffice for your punishment. I will hang you on a cross, alive, until I hear confession of this outrage. Thus I will teach you the true reward of greed.

GUARD
My lord, may I speak?

CREON
Do you not realize that even your voice now offends?

GUARD
My good lord, is it your ears that suffer, or your heart?

CREON
Is it your bravery or your stupidity that keeps you here?

GUARD
Your pardon, my lord. But with leave: The guilty one vexes your heart. I am innocent, though I bother your ears.

CREON
If my enemies could be defeated by babble, you would be my greatest champion.

GUARD
So long as you judge me not guilty of this crime.

CREON
You judge riches more sweet than duty.

GUARD
Alas! That the judge most high should misjudge so badly.

CREON
Bring me the doer of this deed or pay the price with your life.
   (CREON exits.)

GUARD
Well may he be found! But, be he caught or be he not, truly you will not see me here again. Saved now, beyond hope, lowly man that I am, I owe the gods my life.
   (The GUARD exits.)

CHORUS
What do we know of the life of Man,
Most wondrous creature beneath the sky?
Even Earth, the oldest of gods,

Does the human being subdue.
We trap the sea-brood of the deep.
Caught in the meshes of our snares.
We hunt the forests for our meat.

We think thoughts as swift as wind,
And create the rules that make a state,
And cures to ease the dreaded plague,
And shelter from the sun and rain
All of these spring from the mind of Man,
Only Death brings us flat defeat.

Yet still our cunning, fertile minds
Go now to evil, now to good.
Cling we to the rule of law
And walk in rhythm with the gods,
Proudly then our city thrives.
Reject we he who dwells with sin,
And keep us on the narrow path!
  (Enter the GUARD leading ANTIGONE with her wrists bound.)

LEADER
Hard-hearted gods, what means this? Antigone bound? You leave my soul amazed. Hapless child of hapless father, did you recklessly conspire and madly brave the king's decree?

GUARD
Here is the culprit taken in the act. I discovered this girl spreading earth again on Polyneices. Where is the king?
  (CREON enters.)

LEADER
Here comes he from the palace. His timing as inevitable as fate.

CREON
What is it? What has chanced, that makes my coming timely?

GUARD

No man, my lord, should make vows hastily, for on second thought, we oft repent. I had sworn never to show my face here again, having felt the dread of your wrath. And yet here I am, happy as a man with a skin full of wine. I do appear freely before you, bringing this maid who proves I took no part in breaking your decree. She is the one. She alone showed grace to the dead. And I, all eager to clear my name, bring her back to you. Take her. Examine her. But I beseech you now for a free and final quittance from your wrath.

CREON

How and where did you take her?

GUARD

She was in the act. She was sprinkling her brother with soil.

CREON

Do you know what you are saying? You accuse a daughter of the House of Laius?

GUARD

I accuse nothing. I just tell you what I saw.

CREON

Tell me exactly.

GUARD

It happened as such, Your Mercy. No sooner had I returned to Polyneices, flying from your awful threats, than straight we swept away all trace of dust, and bared the clammy body again to the elements. We sat us down on the brow of the hill to the windward of the stench, while each man kept his fellow alert and slapped the sluggard if he chanced to nap. So went it, until the sun's bright orb stood mid heaven, and the heat began to burn. A sudden whirlwind upraised a cloud of dust that blotted out the sky and swept the plain. It stripped the woodlands bare. We closed our eyes and waited till the plague should pass, not one of us suspecting that those gods—divine Helios or mighty Boreas—should desire to intercede. And yet, when sun and wind allowed us sight again, lo! there stood this maid. She cried the cry of a mother bird that finds her nest robbed of chicks. Seeing the corpse bare, but not seeing us who watched, straightway she gathered handfuls of dust and crowned the dead. We rushed forward and seized our quarry, who made no attempt at flight. We questioned and accused her, but she denied nothing, Your Mercy. I was both happy and grieved, for it is sweet to escape threatened doom. Yet to bring disaster to one such as she is most grievous.

CREON
And you, girl. Do you avow or disavow this deed?

ANTIGONE
It is as he said.

CREON
(to GUARD)
You may go, free of guilt.

GUARD
All blessings on Your Worship. And may you find mercy in your heart for this girl.
(Exit GUARD)

CREON
Now answer plain: Had you heard my edict?

ANTIGONE
How could I not?

CREON
And yet you broke the law?

ANTIGONE
Let me ask you, Uncle: Are you more high than Zeus? More profound than holy Justice below? Your mortal breath cannot overrule the laws of Heaven. Their jurisdiction is forever. Should I prefer your laws, I provoke the wrath of Hades and doom my brother's soul to wander. I knew that I must die. Had you not proclaimed it? Yet when one lives surrounded by sorrow, death is bliss. To leave my brother unburied, I would rather be dead. If you judge me foolish in this, it may be you are the fool.

LEADER
Too proud your tongue, Antigone! Better to beg for mercy than to enrage those who love you.

CREON
Enough! Stubborn daughter of a stubborn sire, she glories in her wickedness. If she can flout the law unpunished, then she is king and I am the niece. Bring forth Ismene. I saw her in the palace, frenzied and distraught. A guilty mind oft betrays the doer. Go all and bring her. I would have a word alone with my sister's child.
  (Exit CHORUS.)

ANTIGONE
Would you do more, Uncle, than execute me?

CREON
It is because I do not wish to see you die that I sent the others away. And Haemon means to marry you. I do not care to disappoint my son, either.

ANTIGONE
Perhaps your law is not so absolute.

CREON
Perhaps you are not so stubborn when there is no audience.

ANTIGONE
What will you have of me, Uncle? In truth, I do not wish to be put to death.

CREON
Good. Then you must condemn your crime publicly and stay away from your brother's body.

ANTIGONE
I will do as you ask, but only if you allow Ismene or Haemon—or you yourself—to give Polyneices a burial.

CREON
I cannot show piety towards the one who attacked our city.

ANTIGONE
He is your nephew.

CREON
Did he show piety in killing his own brother?

ANTIGONE
It is not for us to judge his life. He deserves the rites of death.

CREON
Polyneices died our enemy. He killed Eteocles.

ANTIGONE
And what of Eteocles? What about his vow to share the throne? If he had not refused to give Polyneices his turn as king, neither one nor the other would lie low today. A year hence Eteocles would have been on the throne again.

CREON
Eteocles saw the weakness in divided power. And he was right. A leader must show strength. I offered Polyneices my counsel in this dispute: I told him to be the power behind the throne, as I once was to Oedipus.

ANTIGONE
You abetted the arrogance of Eteocles? Then their blood is on your hands, as well!

CREON
Eteocles was the stronger leader. A king makes decisions for the good of the realm.

ANTIGONE
Was it good for the realm that they are dead? I will not trade my brother's soul for the good of the realm. I will condemn my crime, as you ask, but only if Polyneices is buried.

CREON
Antigone. I do not want to condemn you.

ANTIGONE
I cannot sacrifice his soul for my life.

CREON
But after a crime like his, can you hope that he will enter the Elysian Fields? Is it not more likely that your brother be condemned to Tartarus? Is it so much worse that his soul wander here?

ANTIGONE
You cannot know my brother's fate. His journey through Hades' lands is his alone. The one thing we know for certain is that he will never reach the Elysian Fields if left unburied here.

CREON
Perhaps it could be done. Many have fallen in this squabble. We could drag in some slave's body to replace your brother. I will let you do your rites in secret. In exchange, you must publicly condemn your crime and your brother's crime. You must give public support to my law and pledge that no one ever hear of our secret dealings.

ANTIGONE
I will do what you ask, except I cannot condemn
Polyneices at the same time I bury him.

CREON
You need not say his name. Merely gesture to the body of
the slave.

ANTIGONE
I cannot take part in such a conjurer's trick.

CREON
Is your brother now so recognizable? My guards report he
gives forth ripe odor.

ANTIGONE
That is not my objection.

CREON
I offer you life and your brother honor.

ANTIGONE
Public condemnation? A clandestine burial? Where is the
honor in this?

CREON
The honor lies in doing the public good. Bury your brother in secret! It is our fate to rule. We cannot reveal everything we know! There are those in this city who would
dispose of us now.

ANTIGONE
Words carry power. I cannot condemn him in public and
bury him in private. Dark Hades would not accept his
soul. Let me just condemn my crime. Let Ismene bury our
brother.

CREON
Not even Ismene must know of this. And words do carry

power. That is why you must condemn your act and your brother to the people. I cannot show a wavering hand.

ANTIGONE
I will not show a wavering heart.

CREON
Think again. I offer you life.

ANTIGONE
At the price of betraying my brother's soul forever.

CREON
The gods will know what is in your heart.

ANTIGONE
The gods will hear the words from my mouth.

CREON
I give you the chance to save your life. Take it!

ANTIGONE
You think everyone can lie so convincingly? I cannot do it!

CREON
It is not a lie to remain silent. I ask for a simple act, and then you can live and marry Haemon. Don't you want to taste the fullness of life and grow old? Or if your devotions have become so strong, devote your life to the temple of Hades. But first you must correct your defiance of the law.

ANTIGONE
We are the last of a family destroyed by the gods. They will not accept an approximation of their due. If I condemn him, it will contaminate his funeral rites. Then what will be our reckoning?

CREON
You sour the love I feel for you. Go with your brothers to the land of the dead if you must. While I live, I shall not be overthrown by the spawn of Oedipus.
   (Enter ISMENE and CHORUS.)

CHORUS
Creon, King, we bring forth Ismene, shedding such tears as fond sisters weep. A shadow clouds her face, and sorrow staggers her graceful step.

CREON
And you, Niece, did you, too, slink like a viper in my house, to rise suddenly against my throne?

ISMENE
I have done the deed. I share the guilt.

ANTIGONE
Justice will not have this. You would not consent to the deed when I asked your help.

ISMENE
But you are my last love. I walked with you as we tended our blind and beaten father. I will not abandon you now.

ANTIGONE
Whose deed this was, Hades and the dead know well.

ISMENE
Do not scorn me. Let me die with you, and honor the dead.

ANTIGONE
You cannot share in a deed already done.

ISMENE
I feared this moment would come. I thought to remain behind. I pledged to decency that I would perform your

funeral rites. But now that you are condemned, I haven't the strength. Forgive me, sister. I have no taste to remain in this world.

ANTIGONE
Live and see to my burial. Be a comfort to Haemon.

ISMENE
Please, sister.

ANTIGONE
Save yourself. Live and remember me.

ISMENE
This is too much sorrow!

ANTIGONE
We each made our choice.

ISMENE
That was before this final blow.

ANTIGONE
Be of good cheer and live. I was dead already.

CREON
Save yourself, Ismene. Your sister refuses to show the wit for self-survival.

ISMENE
When such misfortune comes, even the wisest lose their mother wit.

CREON
It takes not much wisdom to see how to stay alive.

ISMENE
But how can you execute Antigone? She is promised to your son.

CREON
She cannot be Death's handmaiden and Haemon's wife.

LEADER
Must you deprive your son of his bride?

CREON
What would you have me do?

LEADER
Let her repent and live.

CREON
Ask her yourself. She stands convicted and unrepentant, by her own mouth.

LEADER
Antigone, your gracious king asks you to repent. Will you not save your own life?

ANTIGONE
I would that I could. I cannot live at the expense of my brother's soul.

CREON
You hear with your own ears.
   (To the two attendants)
Delay no more. Take them within and guard them. Even the bravest try to escape when Death draws near.
   (Attendants exit, guarding ANTIGONE and ISMENE. CREON remains.)

CHORUS
Thrice blest are they who never taste evil.
When a house is heaven-shaken, sorrow
Attends forevermore. Hera cursed
Laius with a curse so everlasting,
Every generation suffers all the
More. The oracle told Laius that his

Future son would kill him. He took his love
With men and left his marriage bed cold.

Child-hungry Jocasta gave to Laius
A strong potion, addling his senses,
Putting fire in his loins. From this dark
Night was born the child Oedipus, whom
Laius cast out on a mountainside to
Die. A shepherd found the boy and carried
Him to Corinth where he grew up as the
King's son, proud and rash and strong. Laius
Met Oedipus, traveling for his fortune.
Stepping on a narrow bridge, neither
Man would yield. For a trick of pride, the
Two men came to blows. The son, he killed his
Father, thinking him a stranger. He traveled
On to Thebes, strange city of his birth. The
Blood of Laius forever stained his hands.

Oedipus became king, and husband to
Jocasta. He sired on his mother sibling
Boys and girls. From this sin rose a curse
Upon the city Thebes. The plague afflicted
All till Oedipus found destruction, now his
Sons are dead. His daughters suffer. What can
Happen more? Oh Zeus, we pray you leave us.
Touch us not. Do not exalt us. Nothing
Of your power comes without a curse.

LEADER

Here comes one who has reason for grief.
   (Enter HAEMON)

CREON

Haemon, my son, by now you have heard the pronouncement against the life of your bride. Do you mean to rage against me? Or do I have still your good will, knowing that whatever I have done has been out of love for our family and our state?

HAEMON
Father, you are the patriarch of us all. You govern the city as you govern my youth. No marriage is more precious to me than your good guidance.

CREON
We have lost your brother Megareus. You are the last joy of my age, and it is for you that I feel the strongest grief. Yet ill fares a husband mated with a shrew. This one glories in disobedience. What the king ordains must be obeyed. The rule of law protects the city. I cannot yield to my niece's will, and she will not yield to the law.

LEADER
To us, unless sorrow has dulled our wits, the king's words sound both reasonable and wise.

HAEMON
Wisdom is the choicest gift of heaven. I would not challenge your wisdom, father, even if I could. And yet wise thoughts may come to other men. But you, father, would never hear them. The people would never tell you that which might offend. I overhear when they speak plain and honest. The people mourn this maiden. They say a noble deed has doomed her to her death.

CREON
(gesturing him to come away)
This news, my son, is better told in private.

HAEMON
And yet I believe your justices might confirm what I say. The people sympathize with this girl who saved her brother's body from defilement. For who would allow the eyes of their blood relatives to be plucked by vultures? Their spirit to wander, never to find its kin in the underworld? Would not you bury me, even if I had died in some act of foolish crime? This is not my voice, Father, but the people's, whom I hear in numbers. I take pride in you and

your wisdom. It is for this reason that I ask you to reconsider. The trees that bend before a storm are saved, but those that resist are torn up root and branch. Relent then, Father, and free Antigone. The wisest man will listen to wise advice.

LEADER

Noble king, we deem there is reason in his words. And you, Haemon, can profit by your father's. Both have spoken well.

CREON

He knows little yet of the burdens of statecraft.

HAEMON

Then teach me, Father.

CREON

Would you honor those who undermine the state?

HAEMON

I offer no respect for traitors.

CREON

Except Antigone.

HAEMON

No one in Thebes believes her to be a traitor.

CREON

Shall I ask each man in Thebes to tell me how to rule?

HAEMON

Listen to those you can trust.

CREON

I listen to more than you know. I hear those who would have us fail—those who hate all descendants and relatives of Laius. I must stand firm and rule. We are the law.

HAEMON
We are also family. Can you not do this for your own son?

CREON
I would that I could. But here, in the public square, the city must come first.

HAEMON
No city belongs to one man.

CREON
It takes a firm ruler to protect the city.

HAEMON
The city that needs protection from its ruler is less safe yet.

CREON
You would do better not to chide me in public, boy.

HAEMON
The great ruler knows when to dispense mercy!

CREON
There will be no mercy if I allow chaos to rule.

HAEMON
Civic order will disintegrate if we incur the displeasure of the gods. You know that, Father.

CREON
I know things that you do not. Every man feels righteous when he says the name of God. My city is favored by one god. Their city by another. And because of this we throw spears through one another. I make my sacrifices to the gods. And I make sacrifices for the good of the city. Personal sacrifices! You have no idea what it means to rule!

HAEMON
Then teach me.

CREON
Let us speak in private.

HAEMON
I cannot speak quietly while Antigone is led away.

CREON
Will you give me no opportunity to guide you?

HAEMON
Will you take guidance from no one but yourself? Will you be as stubborn as Uncle Oedipus?

CREON
Then close your ears, fool, if you cannot come away! You will never marry this girl on this side of the grave.

HAEMON
If she must die, her death will destroy another.

CREON
Are you so bold as to make me threats?

HAEMON
How can I threaten ears that are shut tight?

CREON
Were you not my son, you would not still be speaking.

HAEMON
Are you the only man allowed speech in all Thebes? Glorious Thebes, where all are safe, except from the moods of our king!

CREON
I asked you to bring your griefs to me in private. But you cannot resist making speeches for my justices. Your

promised bride taunted me, and so you must taunt me, too! In public. Now, by the gods, you can witness her death.
   (To attendants.)
Bring forth my miserable niece that she may die in his presence, before his eyes, at her bridegroom's side!

HAEMON
I will not stay for your revolting exhibition. Save your speeches for your spineless justices. They are the only ones that can endure you.
   (Exit HAEMON)

LEADER
Wait, Haemon! Call him, good king. A youthful mind, when stung, is fierce.

CREON
Let him go vent his fury! He will not save these two girls from death.

LEADER
Surely you do not mean to slay them both?

CREON
No. You are right. Not her whose hands are clean.

LEADER
And how is the other to die?

CREON
That demands consideration. We will not directly execute her and put that stain upon the state. She shall be taken to some desert place. There she will be sealed in a rock-hewn cave with food for as long as she cares to live. Let her call on Hades. Perhaps he will release her. Or perhaps she will learn too late that love is wasted when spent upon the dead.
   (CREON exits.)

CHORUS
Invincible Love, no one can resist
Your glance, nor arms can fight you as you lie
In wait upon the tender cheek of a maid,
Or wander over land or sea or sky.
Mortal nor immortal can escape.
Yielding to your charm, we all run mad.

By Love, the will of the mighty is bent awry.
The just becomes unjust. So here we see
A love-stirred fight 'tween son and sire and fate
Against the loss of dark Antigone.
When Aphrodite is on the throne, every
Man bends his heart unto her will.
    (ANTIGONE enters, led by attendants.)

LEADER
Not even I can remain on the side of justice
When I see this maid, nor keep dry my
Eyes from streaming tears. Antigone,
So young, so bold, passing thus from the bridal
Chamber to be married to her tomb.

ANTIGONE
Friends, to you my last farewell. My life's
Short journey here is nearly done. I turn
My face now one long last lingering time
Into the sun's dear warmth. I feel already
Gone, for Death puts young and old to sleep.
He calls for me now, too, without a thought
For that which I will miss: Not to marry.
Not to hear the wedding song sung
For me nor see the petals upon my bridal
Bed. Instead, tis Hades I go to wed.

CHORUS
Great and glorious you go to the dead. Unmarkéd

By the wounds of war, withered not
By dread disease, freely you walk, healthy
And fair, like a goddess to the deep.

ANTIGONE

The glory you see is a trick of the eye. The fate
That awaits is like to Niobe's, Tantalus' child.
As ivy grows upon a tree, so to
Stone she slowly turned. And now she's drenched
By pelting rain, left there to pine. And from
Her eyes her tears do flow to frozen breast
Down cheeks of hard, unfeeling rock. Such long
Slow death is like the fate awaiting me.

CHORUS

Yet she was born of gods, divine. You are
Mortal, of mortal line. Oh, holy girl!
For one like you to share the doom of a goddess
Divine will bring you fame forever after.

ANTIGONE

You mock me now in my final hour? Instead
Cry out against this deed! Is justice served?

CHORUS

Too bold, too proud you flaunt the law, and now
Her revenge is horrible, extreme. Yet tis more likely
Some older sin now brings this harsh and bitter
Doom: The curse that follows all your breed.

ANTIGONE

Here you touch on my bitterest thought. My grandfather's
Curse, my unfortunate father, unlucky siblings,
We four are fruit of incestuous sheets. Despised
By the gods, they suffer us not to walk long on the land.
And so I pass, accursed and unwed, to meet
My miserable sires below. How fateful: the acts
Of my brother twins deal me this final deathblow!

CHORUS
Yet do not cast aside all blame. Let rites
Be paid when rites are due. But kings cannot
Hold sway without obeisance to their laws.
All this you know. Tis by your act and not
Your fate you bring pronouncement of your doom.

ANTIGONE
All your words mean naught to me: unwept
Unwed, unloved. The day's bright eye will I
Miss most in Hades realm of eternal night.
   (CREON enters from the palace.)

CREON
If lamentations could stave off death, we would never hear the end. Away with her. Wall her up in a rock-vaulted tomb. Leave her at liberty to die, or, if she choose, to live in solitude, the tomb her dwelling. In either case, we are guiltless of her blood. But she will not again see the light of day.

ANTIGONE
Should I linger in a prison, surrounded by cold rock, shut away in the dark forever? I would rather join those that Persephone has received among the dead. Most miserable fate. And yet I hope that I shall find a welcome from my father, my mother, and my dear Polyneices. These three have my hands washed in their deaths. I dressed their limbs. I poured libations on their graves. And for these sacred duties, I am paid by death. Yet I honored them without fear, and the wise will deem I did so rightly. But now all you, the people of my city, and my king: You judge me guilty. You condemn me. My friends desert me, and I go to a living grave. Can I look to any god for pity? Call on any man for help? Oh, that piety should be deemed criminal. If such justice be approved by heaven, we shall all be taught suffering for our sins.

CHORUS
Such a tempest drives this maiden's soul. Cannot her life be spared even now, oh King?

CREON
Enough. Escort her away, for both our sakes.

ANTIGONE
Uncle, can you not spare me one moment more to look upon my city? Indeed, I would not die. Tis bitter in the end, and I do not wish it. Is there no hope?

CREON
What hope can I offer that you do not already refuse?

ANTIGONE
I condemn my crime, Uncle! I condemn my pride. Only let my brother be buried, and let me live!

LEADER
You break your uncle's heart. You cannot condemn your crime and in the same breath ask it to be repeated.

ANTIGONE
Oh city of my home, Thebes divine! Oh ye gods! Eldest of our race, look upon me, the last of all your royal house! My people, do not forsake me. Understand this of my great and miserable family: Death is the realm of the House of Laius. Made powerful by the gods, we charted the course of our city's life. We carry the burden of rule. And our reward is most bitter. If there be recompense, it must be with Hades. How could I abandon my brother after his short and violent life? Hades is our master. Look what I suffer for his sake, because I would not forget his due! Never to embrace my husband as his wife. Never to feel my baby at my breast. Never again to taste of joy or feel the sun upon my face. Oh, miserable Antigone! I feel as though I have never been awake! How the breeze touches the flesh of my arms, as though this skin never

felt sensation before. How bright the light illumines all around me. Your faces, my friends, shine forth. I smell the astringence of thyme on the hillside—and baking bread on a nearby hearth. Far off I hear children playing. All this to be shut away. No breeze, no light, no sounds but my own sobs. No aroma but damp rock. If this must be my fate, delay no longer, for the richness of this life breaks my heart.

(At a signal from CREON, ANTIGONE is led away by the guards.)

CHORUS (Group A)
Dreadful is the power of Fate. Not wealth,
Nor men at arms, nor walls, nor ships of wood
That breast the sea can stave her off. Thus can
Two men both firm and right stand face to face
With gods defending both, and doubt-free slay
The foe of god, no pity each to each.

CHORUS (Group B)
Where one is right, the other must be wrong.
Righteousness and single vision doth arm
The hand of Man. It takes no pause to see
The view that others hold so dear, and life
Itself is cheaply spent, small coins to throw
Into the font, the wishing well of Fate.

CHORUS (Group A)
Yet must the gods be always honored, this
We know is true. Above all else the gods
Do hold our fate within their hands. Their power
Alone protect us from foes at every
Hand. Therefore must we please them, else
Alone we all do stand.

CHORUS (Group B)
Madness, deafness,
Blindness, these the tools of gods that make
Us miss the haunted cries of fellow man.

What need we hear the truth when high we lift
Our holy righteous cause? Then cry we all:

>(Alternating groups of CHORUS – A & B)

A: The gods are on our side!
B: The gods are on our side!
A: The gods are on our side!
B: The gods are on our side!
>(Enter TEIRESIAS, led by a BOY.)

TEIRESIAS

The gods do speak, Justices of Thebes, but few have ears that open to their words. The rest listen to voices of their own imagining and say: I hear and do your will, oh Lord. Behold two wayfarers of most sensitive ears, but who have betwixt us eyes for only one.

CREON

What are your tidings, agéd Teiresias?

TEIRESIAS

I will tell you. And you must listen with open ears.

CREON

I have never ignored your counsel.

TEIRESIAS

Therefore did you pilot the ship of State aright.

CREON

I know it, and I gladly own my debt.

TEIRESIAS

Mark now you navigate once again the straits of peril.

CREON

What do you mean?

TEIRESIAS

You shall hear: Sitting at my seat of divination, as is my habit, I listened to the birds fly freely and sing. Every species of bird flies there. Their songs bring me both the harmony and the strife of nature, for birds, like humans, do not always live in peace. But then I began to hear weird cries, squawking. Some evil incited in them a frenzy. They tore at one another with beak and claw, wings whirring, suddenly murderous. It filled me with foreboding. Straightaway I lit the fire for sacrifice and bled the lamb. The flames raged on the altar, and we lay the creature atop. The fire embraced its body, but did not devour it as we expected. Instead a putrid slime dripped and sputtered in the ashes. Bladders cracked and spurted gall. The fat melted but would not burn. It peeled away and left the thighbones bare. Hephaistos, God of Fire, had refused to consume our offering.

These signs I saw, related to me by the boy, who wept as he saw the effect on my face. I was filled with terror, for all around the city, the gods reject our rituals. The State is sick, my king, and your new-made law is the worm. Our shrines are profaned, spattered with the regurgitations of vultures that glut themselves on the flesh of Oedipus's son. The birds, gorged with the carnival of human gore, go sick and mad. Therefore do the angry gods abominate our prayers.

Take heed, my lord: The displeasure of the divine is a mightier foe than ten thousand men at arms. A man's decree, though he be a mighty king, is naught but words writ in dust. The gods' laws are eternal. I speak frankly and for your own good.

CREON

You speak for my own good? It is not many days that your words deprived me of my eldest son, my most beloved. Would but one noble Theban give his life freely, so you said, the city would be saved. And so did my son Megareus, the comfort of my age, my heir.

TEIRESIAS
And so the city was saved.

CREON
And so the city was robbed of its best hope for its future king.

TEIRESIAS
I never suggested it need to be Megareus. He took this burden upon himself.

CREON
But he would not have done so had you told me your prophecy in private.

TEIRESIAS
I am a seer, my lord. I am he who brings that which is secret into view. We have had enough die, my king. Let death disarm your vengeance. When someone has been killed, do you stab him again? You must show the full measure of the nobility shown by your noble son.

CREON
Shall I too fall upon my sword? Shall I throw up my rule? Shall I create laws and make them meaningless? Let it be heralded to the mob: Obey or disobey what law you will, for in Thebes the king is weak.

TEIRESIAS
You are but young in rule, my king, and do not yet understand the varieties of strength.

CREON
And you would instruct me aright. Right off my throne. Old man, let fly your shafts at me. I am a favorite target of soothsayers. Who pays you to undermine my reign? No matter how much you amass, you will never purchase this man's burial. Not even if monstrous eagles carry torn chunks of Polyneices to Zeus himself will I permit his

internment. Be ashamed, Teiresias, to practice in deception for coin.

CREON *[sic]*

TEIRESIAS
Of all the fools, the greatest fool is he who will not save himself.

CREON
My concern is for my city.

TEIRESIAS
And yet you show pride in your stubbornness. Do you not remember what stubbornness brought Oedipus?

CREON
Oedipus was brought down by a curse of which I have no part.

TEIRESIAS
No part? Whose son do you refuse to bury? Whose daughter do you condemn? My blindness is nothing compared to yours, for yours is a prideful, self-willed stupidity.

CREON
I will not trade jibes with the seer.

TEIRESIAS
You have already accused me of selling my voice.

CREON
Soothsayers have always been fond of money.

TEIRESIAS
And what of tyrants? What love they?

CREON
Be careful, Teiresias. You speak to your king.

TEIRESIAS
I know it well. I put you on your throne.

CREON
I deny not your wisdom. But now you betray it for coin.

TEIRESIAS
I hoped to spare you, but there is more yet that you have not heard.

CREON
Speak away. Only expect no money from me.

TEIRESIAS
I expect none. Though indeed you shall pay.

CREON
Go stretch out your palm to my enemies. But tell them their gold succeeds only in transforming a trusted seer to a charlatan.

TEIRESIAS
Here, King of Fools: Receive your last prophecy. You shall not live long before you pay with the blood of your own blood in quittance of your blasphemy. You have entombed a living soul, sent below a citizen of the earth before her time. You have wronged the nether gods by leaving here a corpse unwept, unwashed, unsepulchered. Not even the gods in heaven dare refuse Hades' due. Therefore the avenging Furies of the darkest abyss already swirl in the air towards you, that you may taste of these self-same torments. Consider now whether my prophecy be falsified for gold. Wait for the proof, fool, for soon the sound of lamentation shall ring through your desolate halls. These are the shafts that, like a bowman provoked to anger, I loosen at your breast. You shall not dodge their heads. Boy, lead me home, that the king may vent his spleen on sycophantic men, and learn to curb his tongue when wisdom comes to speak.

(The BOY leads TEIRESIAS out.)

CREON
Do not return, Teiresias, until you learn to give the honor

a king is due.
(To the LEADER)
And yet do I feel a powerful unease at his words. What think you, old friend?

LEADER
Ever since his raven hair has turned to white, never have I known the prophet's warning to be false.

CREON
I know it too, and it unsettles the very ground beneath my feet. I remember now the screams of Oedipus: His bloody face, his eyes gouged out with my sister's brooch, by his own hand. The obstinate soul who fights with Fate suffers beyond the tolerance of man.

LEADER
King Creon, listen to advice.

CREON
What should I do? Speak. I will obey.

LEADER
Go, free the maiden from her rocky chamber and make a tomb for her unburied brother.

CREON
You would have me yield?

LEADER
The wise ship's pilot realigns his course when the storm comes. No man sees this as weakness.

CREON
How reluctant I have been to change my resolve. I should look like a fool to reverse my very first command as king. My enemies will see the weakness. But human enemies are nothing compared to the enmity of gods. Only a fool battles Fate. I will make it so.

LEADER
Go. Trust not these deeds to others, but oversee it yourself.

CREON
Everyone, my servants, my citizens, get the axes and tools! Away! It was I that bound her. I will set her free. Panic rises on my heels. How could I put myself above decency?

(CREON and his servants exit.)

LEADER
Who will cure the general sickness and blow the stain from our land? Let us all invoke Thebes patron. Lord Dionysos, evoe! He who dies and is reborn. He who blesses with holy madness. He drives insane those who despise him. Let him never be ignored.

CHORUS
Thou by many names adored,
Child of Zeus the God of thunder,
Fair Italia's guardian lord,
Of a Theban bride the wonder.
Dionysos, evoe!

In the deep-embosomed glades
Of the fair Eleusinian Queen
Haunt of revelers, men and maids,
Dionysos, thou art seen.
Evoe, evoe!

Where the Dragon's teeth were sown,
Where the Maenads are thy daughters
Round ye there we make our home.
Thebes, Oh Bacchus, drinks thy waters.
Dionysos, evoe!

Thou art seen where torches glare.

There to thee thy hymn rings out,
On dark crests of twin peaks bare,
And through our streets we Thebans shout,
Evoe, evoe!

CHORUS

As thou loves our city Thebes,
Home of Semele thy mother,
Listen to our dire needs.
See'st what a plague we're under.
Dionysos, evoe!

Harken now, thy help we crave.
Come, thy frenzied riot bring.
We'll shout and dance thy praises brave.
Refuse us not, but hear us sing:
Evoe, evoe!
   (Enter MESSENGER)

MESSENGER

Attend, all you Thebans. After today, I will despise or envy no man. Fortune plays her games with us all. King Creon I thought a blessed man. He saved the land from enemies and ruled the state supreme—the glorious father of princely children. Now all is waste. What is a life without joys but a living death? He has wealth and praise and power, but if these give no pleasure, a happy peasant is his better.

LEADER

What new griefs have you to tell us?

MESSENGER

Both dead, and they who live deserve to die.

LEADER

Who is dead? And who has killed them? Speak your story plain.

MESSENGER
Haemon is dead. His blood shed by no stranger's hand.

LEADER
Not by his father?

MESSENGER
No. By his own, in fury with his father for the death of Antigone.

LEADER
Oh, Teiresias, how harshly have you proved your word!

MESSENGER
(Bowing to greet her as EURYDICE enters.)
Queen Eurydice.

EURYDICE
People of Thebes, I have heard rumor of news, but I cannot tell you what it is. I went to offer my prayer to Athena. I drew back the bar to open wide the door of her temple and upon my ears there broke a wail. A cry pertaining to some news. I was so stricken with terror, I fainted into my handmaid's arms. What I heard I cannot now remember. Please, if someone knows, tell me what has happened. Let me hear clearly. Do not fear to tell me the truth, for I am no stranger to sorrow.

MESSENGER
Dear mistress, I was there. I will tell you what you wish, though it breaks my heart to do so. I attended the king as we crossed the plain to its farthest edge. There the corpse of Polyneices, horribly mauled by carrion beasts, lay upon the earth. We offered a prayer to Hades and Hecate that they might accept his soul and be merciful to our state. We washed the corpse with proper ceremony. We laid it on a funeral pyre and burned his remains. Afterwards, we buried the ashes with a mighty mound of his native soil. All this we did with our desire for haste battling our need

for proper ceremony. Then to the cavernous rock, to the bridal chamber of Antigone, we sped. But as we drew near, a cry of lamentation broke on every ear. A sob broke in my throat, too, oh Queen, for I recognized your son's cry and the deep grief it carried. The king cried out in his anguish: "Oh, miserable! This is my son's cry."

EURYDICE
Haemon! What has he done?

MESSENGER
The king shouted: "Run! Make haste to the tomb. Tell me is that Haemon's voice, or is this some trick of the gods?" We ran like those pursued by wolves and saw the most sorrowful sight I have ever seen. In the cavern's vaulted gloom, there hung the maiden Antigone, strangled, a noose of linen twined around her neck. I watched as Haemon drew forth his sword and cut her down. He cried her name aloud, as if he would call her back from Hades' realm. He put his ear to her mouth and to her heart, but no breath stirred, no pulse throbbed. Haemon clasped her cold form to him and bewailed the loss of his valiant bride. And then, grief turning to fury, he railed against his father's cold law.

EURYDICE
Oh, Haemon! Oh, my son!

MESSENGER
When the king saw him holding the pitiful body of poor Antigone, he let out a terrible groan. He rushed toward Haemon, crying: "My son, do not let this horrible mischance strip you of your reason. Come away from this wretched place. Let us make our prayers and sacrifices and make amends."

EURYDICE
But he did not go. My son would not loose his grip of her.

MESSENGER

No. The boy glared at him with terrible eyes, spat in his face, and then, without a word, he plucked his sword from the ground and swung, our king barely leaping out of the way—whereupon the royal guards leapt between them. But wretched Haemon, having missed his chance for vengeance, fell to wailing and staggered to the back of the cave. Then a sudden bitter resolve gripped him. Far too quickly for anyone to stop him, he set his sword's hilt to the ground and fell upon it with all his might...

EURYDICE

No!

MESSENGER

...driving the sword half its length into his side.

EURYDICE

No...

MESSENGER

While he yet breathed, he clasped the maid in his quivering arms, her pallid cheek spattered red with his dying gasps. Then they lay, two corpses, one in death. Now they consummate their marriage vows in the halls of Death. Our king fell to the ground and wept. He demonstrates to all, whatever sorrow befalls mankind, man's arrogance brings the worst.
   (EURYDICE exits)

LEADER

What do you make of this? The Queen goes without a word.

MESSENGER

I would think she goes to lament these new deaths in private. She is a most noble woman. She will do nothing that ill-befits a queen.

LEADER
I am not so certain. Forced silence is no less ominous than excessive tears.

MESSENGER
Perhaps you are right. I will follow her. Unnatural calm may mean no good.
  (MESSENGER exits. Enter CREON with attendants, carrying the shrouded body of HAEMON.)

CHORUS
Lo! The king approaches. He bears the evidence against himself. I fear to make such a charge against a king, but all must recognize, the guilt is his.

CREON
Witness your king, oh Thebes. I am destroyed by the perverse stubbornness of my own will. I abandoned decency to mistreat the dead. Gaze upon us, executioner and victim. Damned by the wretched foolishness of warfare! How could I choose a misguided vigilance over my own son! Look at him: dead, hardly past childhood, through no fault of his own. The fault was mine, mine alone. Oh my son!

LEADER
Miserable king, too late came your repentance to avert the horror of Fate.

CREON
I am most brutally schooled by sorrow. Dark Hades has struck me down, humbled my pride, and transformed my pleasure to pain. We mortals are but the playthings of the gods! All our labor comes to naught!
  (Enter MESSENGER.)

MESSENGER
You are most grievously schooled by trials, my lord, and yet there is more to come, and yet even more sorrowful.

CREON
More sorrowful? It is not possible.

MESSENGER
Your wife, the mother of your sons, lies felled by a fresh inflicted wound.

CREON
What say you? Have I not felt the cold slashes of death already? My sons are dead. I am dead. When a man has been killed, do you stab him again? Nay, I have heard these words before! Who plays tricks with me? My son, do you speak? What say we all? Are we not all already dead? Stroke upon stroke: first Megareus, then Antigone, then Haemon, now Eurydice slain?

CHORUS
Look for yourself. She lies for all to view.
(The corpse of EURYDICE is disclosed.)

CREON
Alas! What remains to crown my agony? I have only now held my blood-drained son in my arms. Unhappy mother, most unhappy son!

MESSENGER
Beside the altar of Athena she fell upon a keen-edged sword and closed her eyes. She mourned Megareus who gave his life for the sake of Thebes, and again for her most unhappy Haemon. I hesitate to speak more, but speak I must, for she made me promise to tell you: With her last breath she cursed you, my lord, whom she blamed for both their deaths.

CREON
More of this I cannot bear. Will no one end my suffering? Send for a sword and dispatch your wretched king. I want no more misery. Both son and mother died of their own hand?

MESSENGER
Hearing the lament begin for Haemon, she stabbed herself to the heart.

CREON
I am the killer. I did the deed, your murder. No one but I. Lead me away and end this miserable life. There is nothing left for your king.

LEADER
And yet you must carry on. Having no son, no heir, you must set your city to rights.

CREON
Come, vengeful gods, be a friend at last. When one lives surrounded by sorrow, death is bliss. Force me not to look upon another day!

CHORUS (Group A)
You must bear with heartbreak, oh King.

CREON
All my desires were summed in that prayer. I want only death.

CHORUS (Group B)
Pray no further. Duty demands you live. Of refuge there is none.

CREON
I know not where to turn. To live with myself, all loved ones gone, is the most bitter sentence of all.

CHORUS (Group B)
When life chooses to punish us, no limit does it set. Punished by Fate, punished by gods, punished by other men, all pains we must endure.

CHORUS (Group A)
And yet most bitter is the penalty we draw upon ourselves. When human strife puts us in conflict with the

gods, most careful must we be.

CHORUS (Group B)
Fear of enemies shakes our dedication to the old laws. Fear blinds us to our need for reverence and decency.

LEADER
Fear blinds us to the true nature of our fellow man. He who cannot understand the dreams of his neighbors will live in blindness. Across the earth he will see only enemies. And yet in their hearts, all men are the same.

CHORUS (Group A)
They long for peace, and for the good of their children. They long to better their families, their cities and themselves. Looking far off, they fathom not what stirs in the hearts of other men.

CHORUS (Group B)
Better to slay them before they attack. Better to thwart the evil before it approaches.

LEADER
But evil sits in all hearts disguised. When we watch for the evil in others, we cease to see it in ourselves.

CHORUS (Group B)
The enemy is always evil, and we are always good. Our acts are always justified.

CHORUS (Group A)
But without reverence for all men, there can be reverence for none. Without reverence for all men, our fate is misery. Without reverence for all men...

LEADER
Antigone dies.

CURTAIN

Glossary & Pronunciation Guide

Antigone /ann-TIG-uh-knee/: The elder daughter of Oedipus and Jocasta.

Aphrodite /af-rah-DIE-tee/: The goddess of love and beauty.

Athena /uh-THEE-nah/: The goddess of wisdom and warfare.

Boreas /BORE-ee-us/: The god of the north wind.

Creon /KREE-ahn/: Brother-in-law (and uncle) of Oedipus, brother of Jocasta.

Dionysos /die-oh-NIGH-suss/: God of wine, madness and inspiration; patron of Thebes and theatre.

Eleusinian /el-you-SIN-ee-an/: Relating to a city near Athens, site of the Eleusinian mysteries.

Elysian Fields /ill LIZH uhn/: The abode of the blessed after death. The 'heaven' of Hades.

Eteocles /eh-TEE-uh-cleez/: Antigone's brother who

would not allow Polyneices his turn on the throne of Thebes.

Eurydice /you-RID-uh-see/: Wife of Creon; mother of Haemon.

Evoe /AY-voe-ay/: A cry of celebration.

Hades /HAY-deez/: God of the Underworld. Also the land of the Underworld.

Haemon /HAY-mahn/: Antigone's fiancé; Creon's son.

Hecate /HECK-ah-tee/: A goddess of the underworld.

Helios /HEE-lee-ahs/: The sun god.

Hephaistos /heh-FESS-tis/: God of Fire.

Ismene /IZ-muh-nay/: Antigone's younger sister.

Jocasta /joe-CASS-tah/: Mother (and wife) of Oedipus; sister of Creon.

Laius /LAY-uss/: Father of Oedipus, whom Oedipus killed.

Maenads /MEE-nads/: Woman members of the orgiastic cult of Dionysos.

Megareus /muh-GAIR-ee-uss/: Creon's oldest son who sacrificed himself before the battle in which Oedipus' sons died.

Oedipus /ED-uh-puss/: Father (and brother) of Antigone and Ismene.

Persephone /purr-SEFF-ah-knee/: wife-queen of Hades.

Antigone

Polyneices /pol-uh-NIGH-sees/: The exiled brother who raised an army against Thebes.

Semele /SAME-ah-lee/: The human mother of Dionysos.

Tantalus /TAN-ta-lis/: A king who was 'tantalized' in Hades for eternity for his crimes.

Tartarus /TAR-ter-iss/: The lowest depths of Hades.

Teiresias /teer-EE-see-uss/: The blind prophet.

Thebes /THEEBZ/: The city.

Absolute Macbeth

Adapted from William Shakespeare's tragedy
by Richard Engling

Three witches cast a circle of magic to the beat of drums and wafts of incense. Like ritual priestesses, they draw in Macbeth, the ambitious warrior who would be king. They flatter his vanity and encourage the evil inside him. And helping it blossom, they allow it to be purged, purifying the Kingdom.

Macbeth is the clang of weaponry, temptation followed by murder, more murder, revenge and retribution.

The Polarity production takes place in ritual space, in a timeless zone where a soul acquiesces to its own destruction. This is Absolute Macbeth, *Shakespeare's words to the rhythm of drums, passion, choreographed battle, and sacrificial rite. It's* Macbeth *done as a sacrament to purge the tyrant from our society.*

The world premiere of *Absolute Macbeth* was presented by Polarity Ensemble Theatre at the Breadline Center for the Performing Arts, 1802 West Berenice, Chicago. It opened April 29, 2005.

Cast, in order of appearance

Drummer, Third Murderer,
    Caithness, Doctor . . . . Eric S. Cartier
Drummer, Porter, Old Man, Old Siward . . . . Daniel Houle
Drummer, Fleance, Apparition II . . . . Zoë Olivia
Drummer, Donalbain, Young Siward . . Timothy Tsurutani
First Witch, Messenger, A Lord . . . . Abigail Trabue
Second Witch, Seyton, A Lord . . . . Patricia Austin
Third Witch, A Lord, Gentlewoman . . . . . . Victoria Gilbert
King Duncan . . . . Peter Esposito
Malcolm . . . . Jason LeCompte
Captain, First Murderer . . . . Mason Hill
Lennox . . . . Rory Leahy
Ross . . . . Charley Jordan
Macbeth . . . . Brent Rivera
Banquo . . . . Steven Marzolf
Lady Macbeth . . . . Ann Keen
Macduff. . . . . Bobby Zaman
Second Murderer . . . . Jason Wisnewski

Antigone & Macbeth

Servant, Apparition I, English Doctor..... Colleen Tutton
Macduff's Son, Apparition III............. Ryan Tutton
Lady Macduff................... Kelly Hoogenakker

Staff

Director ....Richard Engling
Assistant Director ....Zack Brenner
Stage Manager ....Thomas Lesh
Costume Designer ....Amy E. Landes
Lighting Designer ....Tony Ligeza
Scenic Designer ....David Orr
Properties Director ....Wendy Mingin
Fight Choreographer ....David Yondorf
Fight Captain ....Mason Hill
Mask Designer ....Jessica Pribble
Assistant Mask Designer ....Glen Cullen
Master Carpenter ....Miguel Pelayo
Stage Carpenter ....James Engling
Graphic Design ....Cathleen Ann

Please visit www.PETheatre.com for information on a DVD documenting this production.

Absolute Macbeth

Production Notes

Absolute Macbeth takes place in ritual space, outside of any specific time or location. It is a timeless space in which a soul acquiesces to its own destruction, and evil is purged from the community. In the first scene, the witches cast the ritual circle in which the performance takes place. They are ritual priestesses who encourage the evil to come to its full force so that it can be destroyed. In casting the circle, they dance to percussion, burn incense and mark the circle in chalk on the floor. The purgation of Macbeth takes place within that circle.

The witches and other off-stage actors are frequently visible to the audience in positions outside the circle. From outside the circle they play the percussion that marks the scene changes. The scenes including combat and magic are also accompanied by percussion.

Actors who have studied First Folio Technique will be pleased to note that the punctuation used in this text is the same as that used in the First Folio. Shakespeare's original act and scene breaks are shown as well as our own break for a single intermission. The second act of our two act structure begins on page 114.

ACT ONE

Act I

Scene i:

Four percussionists enter from the back of the stage and take their places at the drums, upstage center. The three WITCHES enter from upstage center, downstage right and downstage left. They stand downstage, side by side, and address the audience.

FIRST WITCH

Welcome.

SECOND WITCH

Welcome.

THIRD WITCH

Welcome.
   (They put on masks made from fox face pelts and fur. The PERCUSSIONISTS launch into a heavy tribal beat. The WITCHES dance the circle. They carry ceremonial fans made of bird's wings. The SECOND WITCH uses her fan to brush the full stage with incense smoke as they invoke the four directions. The volume of the drums comes down as they begin the invocation.)

THIRD WITCH
Guardians of the Watchtowers of the East:
O Lords of Air,
I do summon, stir, and call you up,
To observe our rites and to protect the Circle.

FIRST WITCH
Guardians of the Watchtowers of the West:
O Lords of Water,
Lords of Death and Initiation;
I do summon, stir, and call you up,
To observe our rites and to protect the Circle.

THIRD WITCH
Guardians of the Watchtowers of the South,
O Lords of Fire;
I do summon, stir and call you up,
To observe our rites and to protect the Circle.

FIRST WITCH
Guardians of the Watchtowers of the North,
O Lords of Earth;
Boreas, thou gracious protector of the Northern Portals;
I do summon, stir and call you up,
To observe our rites and to protect the Circle.

(Six members of the cast carry in MACBETH on their shoulders like PALLBEARERS. They wear veils over their faces to indicate they are in a ritual role rather than their individual roles. They set MACBETH in the center of the circle. They exit. The WITCHES circle around MACBETH who stands motionless and expressionless. He is the raw material of MACBETH. They anoint him with smoke and dedicate him to the ritual.)

FIRST WITCH
The circle cast: the magic's set,
To cast a man forth for destruction.

SECOND WITCH
To take with him all our corruption,
That surrounds this weal invisibly.

THIRD WITCH
Make seen in him; the gods to feed:
Take him for us, that's what we plead.

FIRST WITCH
   (turning to the west to invoke the goddess)
Mother!

SECOND WITCH
   (likewise)
Mother!

THIRD WITCH
   (likewise)
Mother!

FIRST WITCH
Will it please you eat?

SECOND WITCH
Will it please your godhead feed?

THIRD WITCH
Ha!
   (Drums louder again. The WITCHES whirl around
MACBETH as he exits. The drums come back down as the
WITCHES gather again in the center.)

FIRST WITCH
When shall we three meet again?
In thunder, lightning, or in rain?

SECOND WITCH
When the hurlyburly's done,
When the battle's lost and won.

THIRD WITCH
That will be ere the set of sun.

FIRST WITCH
Where the place?

SECOND WITCH
Upon the heath.

THIRD WITCH
There to meet with Macbeth.

FIRST WITCH
I come, Graymalkin.

ALL
Paddock calls: anon: fair is foul, and foul is fair,
Hover through the fog and filthy air.
    (They exit dancing to loud drumming.)

Act I

Scene ii:

A Camp near Forres. Enter KING DUNCAN, MALCOLM, DONALBAIN and LENNOX from upstage. A bleeding CAPTAIN enters from downstage. Drums subside.

DUNCAN
What bloody man is that? He can report,
As seemeth by his plight, of the revolt
The newest state.

MALCOLM
This is the sergeant,
Who like a good and hardy soldier fought
'Gainst my captivity: Hail brave friend;
Say to the king, the knowledge of the broil,
As thou didst leave it.

Absolute Macbeth

CAPTAIN

Doubtful it stood,
As two spent swimmers, that do cling together,
And choke their art: The merciless Macdonwald,
(Worthy to be a rebel, for to that
The multiplying villainies of nature
Do swarm upon him) from the Western isles
Of kerns and gallowglasses is supplied,
And fortune on his damned quarry smiling,
Show'd like a rebel's whore: but all's too weak:
For brave Macbeth (well he deserves that name)
Disdaining fortune, with his brandish'd steel,
Which smok'd with bloody execution
(Like valor's minion) carv'd out his passage,
Till he fac'd the slave:
And ne'er shook hands, nor bade farewell to him,
Till he unseam'd him from the nave toth' chops,
And fix'd his head upon our battlements.

DUNCAN

O valiant cousin, worthy gentleman.

CAPTAIN

As whence the sun 'gins his reflection,
Shipwrecking storms, and direful thunders:
So from that spring, whence comfort seem'd to come,
Discomfort swells: Mark King of Scotland, mark,
No sooner justice had, with valor arm'd,
Compell'd these skipping kerns to trust their heels,
But the Norweyan lord, surveying vantage,
With furbish'd arms, and new supplies of men,
Began a fresh assault.

DUNCAN

Dismay'd not this our captains, Macbeth and
Banquo?

CAPTAIN

Yes, as sparrows eagles;
Or the hare, the lion:

If I say sooth, I must report they were
As cannons over-charg'd with double cracks,
So they doubly redoubled strokes upon the foe:
Except they meant to bathe in reeking wounds,
Or memorize another Golgotha,
I cannot tell: but I am faint,
My gashes cry for help.

DUNCAN

So well thy words become thee, as thy wounds,
They smack of honor both: go, get him surgeons.
    (Exit CAPTAIN, supported by DONALDBAIN.)
Who comes here?

MALCOLM

The worthy Thane of Ross.

LENNOX

What a haste looks through his eyes?
So should he look, that seems to speak things strange.
    (Enter ROSS.)

ROSS

God save the King.

DUNCAN

Whence cam'st thou, worthy thane?

ROSS

From Fife, great king,
Where the Norweyan banners flout the sky,
And fan our people cold.
Norway himself, with terrible numbers,
Assisted by that most disloyal traitor,
The Thane of Cawdor, began a dismal conflict,
Till that Bellona's bridegroom, lapp'd in proof,
Confronted him with self-comparisons,
Point against point, rebellious arm 'gainst arm,
Curbing his lavish spirit: and to conclude,
The victory fell on us.

DUNCAN

Great happiness.
No more that Thane of Cawdor shall deceive
Our bosom interest: go pronounce his present death,
And with his former title greet Macbeth.

ROSS

I'll see it done.

DUNCAN

What he hath lost, noble Macbeth hath won.
　　(They all exit. Drums. The lights lower.)

Act I

Scene iii:

A heath. Enter the three WITCHES.

THIRD WITCH

A drum, a drum:
Macbeth doth come.

ALL

The weyward sisters, hand in hand,
Posters of the sea and land,
Thus do go, about, about:
Thrice to thine, and thrice to mine,
And thrice again, to make up nine.
Peace, the charm's wound up.
　　(They crouch to hide in waiting, upstage, downstage right and downstage left. Drums fade out as MACBETH and BANQUO enter and cross to center stage.)

MACBETH

So foul and fair a day I have not seen.

BANQUO

How far is't call'd to Forres?

(The WITCHES rise to reveal themselves. MACBETH and BANQUO pull their weapons.)
What are these,
So wither'd, and so wild in their attire,
That look not like th' inhabitants o' th' earth,
And yet are on't? Live you, or are you aught
That man may question? You seem to understand me,
By each at once her choppy finger laying
Upon her skinny lips: you should be women,
And yet your beards forbid me to interpret
That you are so.

MACBETH
Speak if you can: what are you?

FIRST WITCH
All hail Macbeth, hail to thee Thane of Glamis.

SECOND WITCH
All hail Macbeth, hail to thee, Thane of Cawdor.

THIRD WITCH
All hail Macbeth, that shalt be king hereafter.

BANQUO
Good sir, why do you start, and seem to fear
Things that do sound so fair? I' the name of truth
Are ye fantastical, or that indeed
Which outwardly ye show? My noble partner
You greet with present grace, and great prediction
Of noble having, and of royal hope,
That he seems rapt withal: to me you speak not.
If you can look into the seeds of time,
And say which grain will grow, and which will not,
Speak then to me, who neither beg, nor fear
Your favors, nor your hate.

FIRST WITCH
Hail.

Absolute Macbeth

SECOND WITCH
Hail.

THIRD WITCH
Hail.

FIRST WITCH
Lesser than Macbeth, and greater.

SECOND WITCH
Not so happy, yet much happier.

THIRD WITCH
Thou shalt get kings, though thou be none:
So all hail Macbeth, and Banquo.

FIRST WITCH
Banquo, and Macbeth, all hail.
 (They cross to the upstage right platform to exit, but stop as MACBETH addresses them.)

MACBETH
Stay you imperfect speakers, tell me more:
By Sinell's death, I know I am Thane of Glamis,
But how, of Cawdor? The Thane of Cawdor lives
A prosperous gentleman: and to be king,
Stands not within the prospect of belief,
No more than to be Cawdor. Say from whence
You owe this strange intelligence, or why
Upon this blasted heath you stop our way
With such prophetic greeting?
Speak, I charge you.
 (The WITCHES laugh and wave their bird's wing fans in front of them as they crouch to the floor, making themselves invisible to MACBETH and BANQUO. They remain there and watch the rest of the scene.)

BANQUO
The earth hath bubbles, as the water has,
And these are of them: whither are they vanish'd?

MACBETH
Into the air: and what seem'd corporal,
Melted, as breath into the wind.
Would they had stay'd.

BANQUO
Were such things here, as we do speak about?
Or have we eaten on the insane root,
That takes the reason prisoner?

MACBETH
Your children shall be kings.

BANQUO
You shall be king.

MACBETH
And Thane of Cawdor too: went it not so?

BANQUO
To the selfsame tune and words: Who's here?
    (They pull their weapons again as ROSS and LENNOX enter. They all laugh as friends are recognized.)

ROSS
The king hath happily receiv'd, Macbeth,
The news of thy success: and when he reads
Thy personal venture in the rebels' sight,
His wonders and his praises do contend,
Which should be thine, or his.

LENNOX
We are sent
To give thee from our royal master thanks,
Only to herald thee into his sight,
Not pay thee.

ROSS

And for an earnest of a greater honor,
He bade me, from him, call thee Thane of Cawdor:
In which addition, hail most worthy thane,
For it is thine.

BANQUO

What, can the devil speak true?

MACBETH

The Thane of Cawdor lives:
Why do you dress me in borrowed robes?

LENNOX

Who was the Thane, lives yet,
But under heavy judgement bears that life,
Which he deserves to lose.
But treasons capital, confess'd and prov'd,
Have overthrown him.

MACBETH

(Aside.)
Glamis, and Thane of Cawdor:
The greatest is behind. (to Lennox and Ross) Thanks for your pains.
(to Banquo) Do you not hope your children shall be kings,
When those that gave the Thane of Cawdor to me,
Promis'd no less to them?

BANQUO

That trusted home,
Might yet enkindle you unto the crown,
Besides the Thane of Cawdor. But 'tis strange:
And oftentimes, to win us to our harm,
The instruments of darkness tell us truths,
Win us with honest trifles, to betray's
In deepest consequence.
Cousins, a word, I pray you.
    (BANQUO, ROSS and LENNOX cross upstage.)

MACBETH
(Aside.)
Two truths are told,
As happy prologues to the swelling act
Of the imperial theme. (to Lennox and Ross) I thank you gentlemen:
(Aside, downstage center, to the audience.)
This supernatural soliciting
Cannot be ill; cannot be good.
If ill? why hath it given me earnest of success,
Commencing in a truth? I am Thane of Cawdor.
If good? why do I yield to that suggestion,
Whose horrid image doth unfix my hair,
And make my seated heart knock at my ribs,
Against the use of nature? Present fears
Are less than horrible imaginings:
My thought, whose murder yet is but fantastical,
Shakes so my single state of man,
That function is smother'd in surmise,
And nothing is, but what is not.

BANQUO
Look, how our partner's rapt.

MACBETH
(Aside.)
If chance will have me king,
Why chance may crown me,
Without my stir.

BANQUO
New honors come upon him
Like our strange garments, cleave not to their mold
But with the aid of use.

MACBETH
(Aside.)
Come what come may,
Time, and the hour, runs through the roughest day.

BANQUO
Worthy Macbeth, we stay upon your leisure.

MACBETH
Give me your favor:
My dull brain was wrought with things forgotten.
Kind gentlemen, your pains are registred,
Where every day I turn the leaf,
To read them.
Let us toward the king: Think upon
What hath chanc'd: and, at more time,
The interim having weigh'd it, let us speak
Our free hearts each to other.

BANQUO
Very gladly.

MACBETH
Till then, enough:
Come, friends.
    (Drums. All exit, including the WITCHES.)

Act I

Scene iv:

Forres. A Room in the Palace. Enter DUNCAN, MALCOLM, DONALBAIN and FLEANCE.

DUNCAN
Is execution done on Cawdor?
Or not those in commission yet return'd?

MALCOLM
My liege, They are not yet come back.
But I have spoke with one that saw him die:
Who did report, that very frankly he
Confess'd his treasons, implor'd your highness' pardon,

And set forth a deep repentance:
Nothing in his life became him,
Like the leaving it. He died,
As one that had been studied in his death,
To throw away the dearest thing he ow'd,
As 'twere a careless trifle.

DUNCAN

There's no art,
To find the mind's construction in the face.
He was a gentleman, on whom I built
An absolute trust.
   (Enter MACBETH, BANQUO, ROSS, and LENNOX.)
O worthiest cousin,
The sin of my ingratitude even now
Was heavy on me. Thou art so far before,
That swiftest wing of recompense is slow
To overtake thee. Would thou hadst less deserv'd,
That the proportion both of thanks, and payment,
Might have been mine: only I have left to say,
More is thy due, than more than all can pay.

MACBETH

The service, and the loyalty I owe,
In doing it, pays itself.
Your highness' part, is to receive our duties:
And our duties are to your throne, and state,
Children, and servants; which do but what they should,
By doing everything safe toward your love
And honor.

DUNCAN

Welcome hither:
I have begun to plant thee, and will labor
To make thee full of growing. Noble Banquo,
That hast no less deserv'd, nor must be known
No less to have done so, let me enfold thee,
And hold thee to my heart.

BANQUO

There if I grow,
The harvest is your own.

DUNCAN

My plenteous joys,
Wanton in fulness, seek to hide themselves
In drops of sorrow. Sons, kinsmen, thanes,
And you whose places are the nearest, know,
We will establish our estate upon
Our eldest, Malcolm, whom we name hereafter,
The Prince of Cumberland: which honor must
Not unaccompanied, invest him only,
But signs of nobleness, like stars, shall shine
On all deservers. From hence to Inverness,
And bind us further to you.

MACBETH

The rest is labor, which is not us'd for you:
I'll be myself the harbinger, and make joyful
The hearing of my wife, with your approach:
So humbly take my leave.

DUNCAN

My worthy Cawdor.

MACBETH

(Aside, downstage to the audience.)
The Prince of Cumberland: That is a step,
On which I must fall down, or else o'erleap,
For in my way it lies. Stars hide your fires,
Let not light see my black and deep desires:
The eye wink at the hand: yet let that be,
Which the eye fears, when it is done to see.
   (MACBETH exits. Drums. All exit.)

Act I

Scene v:

Inverness. LADY MACBETH'S chamber.
Enter LADY MACBETH, reading a letter. Drums subside.

LADY MACBETH

They met me in the day of success: and I have learn'd by the perfect'st report, they have more in them, than mortal knowledge. When I burnt in desire to question them further, they made themselves air, into which they vanish'd. Whiles I stood rapt in the wonder of it, came missives from the king, who all-hailed me Thane of Cawdor, by which title, before, these weyward sisters saluted me, and referr'd me to the coming on of time, with Hail king that shalt be. This have I thought good to deliver thee (my dearest partner of greatness) that thou might'st not loose the dues of rejoicing by being ignorant of what greatness is promis'd thee. Lay it to thy heart, and farewell.

Glamis thou art, and Cawdor, and shalt be
What thou art promis'd: yet do I fear thy nature,
It is too full o' the milk of human kindness,
To catch the nearest way. Thou wouldst be great,
Art not without ambition, but without
The illness should attend it. What thou wouldst highly,
That wouldst thou holily; wouldst not play false,
And yet wouldst wrongly win.
Thou'dst have, great Glamis, that which cries,
Thus thou must do, if thou have it;
And that which rather thou dost fear to do,
Than wishest should be undone. Hie thee hither,
That I may pour my spirits in thine ear,
And chastise with the valor of my tongue
All that impedes thee from the golden round,
Which fate and metaphysical aid doth seem
To have thee crown'd withal.

Absolute Macbeth

(Enter A MESSENGER. This is WITCH 1, carrying a mask.)
What is your tidings?

MESSENGER (WITCH 1)
The king comes here tonight.

LADY MACBETH
Thou'rt mad to say it.
Is not thy master with him? who, were't so,
Would have inform'd for preparation.

MESSENGER (WITCH 1)
So please you, it is true: our thane is coming:
One of my fellows had the speed of him;
Who almost dead for breath, had scarcely more
Than would make up his message.

LADY MACBETH
Give him tending;
He brings great news.
(Exit MESSENGER. WITCH 1 immediately reenters. WITCH 2 and WITCH 3 enter from downstage left and right. They gather around LADY MACBETH, invisible to her during the following speech. They gather close around her and anoint her with incense smoke. (DIRECTOR'S NOTE: *Macbeth* has the reputation of being a play that plagues the companies that perform it with bad luck. Many actors refer to *Macbeth* as "The Scottish Play" to avoid pronouncing the bad luck title. To my mind, it is much more likely that the bad luck comes not from pronouncing the title of the play, but from reciting lines such as the ones below. In our production, as the WITCHES gathered around LADY MACBETH, seemingly to encourage her wickedness, Trish Austin, the actress playing WITCH 2, was actually pronouncing prayers of protection over Ann Keen's LADY MACBETH and over the company as a whole. Prayers of protection were secretly incorporated into the production in a few strategic moments.))

The raven himself is hoarse,
That croaks the fatal entrance of Duncan
Under my battlements. (She sinks to her knees.) Come you spirits,
That tend on mortal thoughts, unsex me here,
And fill me from the crown to the toe, top-full
Of direst cruelty: make thick my blood,
Stop up the access, and passage to remorse,
That no compunctious visitings of nature
Shake my fell purpose, nor keep peace between
Th' effect and hit. Come to my woman's breasts,
And take my milk for gall, you murdering ministers,
Wherever, in your sightless substances,
You wait on nature's mischief. Come thick night,
And pall thee in the dunnest smoke of hell,
That my keen knife see not the wound it makes,
Nor heaven peep through the blanket of the dark,
To cry, Hold, hold.
  (Enter MACBETH. The WITCHES hiss, swirl and exit, invisible still to both MACBETH and LADY MACBETH. The scene below is played seductively, with LADY MACBETH drawing in her husband when he hesitates.)
Great Glamis, Worthy Cawdor,
Greater than both, by the all-hail hereafter,
Thy letters have transported me beyond
This ignorant present, and I feel now
The future in the instant.

MACBETH
My dearest love,
Duncan comes here tonight.

LADY MACBETH
And when goes hence?

MACBETH
To-morrow, as he purposes.

LADY MACBETH

O, never
Shall sun that morrow see.
Your face, my thane, is as a book, where men
May read strange matters. To beguile the time,
Look like the time; bear welcome in your eye,
Your hand, your tongue: look like th' innocent flower,
But be the serpent under't. He that's coming,
Must be provided for: and you shall put
This night's great business into my dispatch,
Which shall to all our nights, and days to come,
Give solely sovereign sway, and masterdom.

MACBETH

(Reluctant.)
We will speak further.

LADY MACBETH

(Teasing him.)
Only look up clear:
To alter favor, ever is to fear:
Leave all the rest to me.
    (He pursues her offstage. Drums.)

Act I

Scene vi:

The same. Before the Castle. Enter DUNCAN, MALCOLM, DONALBAIN, BANQUO, LENNOX, MACDUFF, ROSS and FLEANCE. Drums subside.

DUNCAN

This castle hath a pleasant seat,
The air nimbly and sweetly recommends itself
Unto our gentle senses.

BANQUO

This guest of summer,
The temple-haunting bartlet does approve,
By his lov'd mansionry, that the heaven's breath
Smells wooingly here: no jutty, frieze,
Buttress, nor coigne of vantage, but this bird
Hath made his pendant bed, and procreant cradle,
Where they most breed, and haunt: I have observ'd
The air is delicate.
    (Enter LADY MACBETH.)

DUNCAN

See, see our honour'd hostess:
The love that follows us, sometime is our trouble,
Which still we thank as love. Herein I teach you,
How you shall bid God ild us for your pains,
And thank us for your trouble.

LADY MACBETH

All our service,
In every point twice done, and then done double,
Were poor, and single business, to contend
Against those honours deep, and broad,
Wherewith your majesty loads our house.

DUNCAN

Where's the Thane of Cawdor?
We cours'd him at the heels, and had a purpose
To be his purveyor: but he rides well,
And his great love (sharp as his spur) hath holp him
To his home before us: Fair and noble hostess,
We are your guest tonight.

LADY MACBETH

Your servants ever,
Have theirs, themselves, and what is theirs in compt,
To make their audit at your highness' pleasure,
Still to return your own.

Absolute Macbeth

DUNCAN

Give me your hand:
Conduct me to mine host: we love him highly,
And shall continue, our graces towards him.
By your leave hostess.
    (They exit. Drums.)

Act I

Scene vii:

The same. A Lobby in the Castle. Enter MACBETH to the upstage right platform. Drums subside.

MACBETH

If it were done, when 'tis done, then 'twere well,
It were done quickly: If the assassination
Could trammel up the consequence, and catch
With his surcease, success: that but this blow
Might be the be-all, and the end-all. Here,
But here, upon this bank and shoal of time,
We'd jump the life to come. (Crosses a few paces downstage) But in these cases,
We still have judgement here, that we but teach
Bloody instructions, which being taught, return
To plague the inventor: this even-handed justice
Commends th' ingredients of our poison'd chalice
To our own lips. (Crosses a few paces downstage) He's here in double trust;
First, as I am his kinsman, and his subject,
Strong both against the deed: then, as his host,
Who should against his murderer shut the door,
Not bear the knife myself. (Crosses to downstage center) Besides, this Duncan
Hath borne his faculties so meek; hath been
So clear in his great office, that his virtues
Will plead like angels, trumpet-tongued against
The deep damnation of his taking-off:

And pity, like a naked new-born babe,
Striding the blast, or heaven's cherubin, hors'd
Upon the sightless couriers of the air,
Shall blow the horrid deed in every eye,
That tears shall drown the wind. (A roar of laughter from offstage). I have no spur
To prick the sides of my intent, but only
Vaulting ambition, which o'erleaps itself,
And falls on the other.
    (Enter LADY MACBETH from upstage left.)
How now? What news?

LADY MACBETH

He has almost supp'd: why have you left the chamber?

MACBETH

Hath he ask'd for me?

LADY MACBETH

Know you not, he has?

MACBETH

We will proceed no further in this business:
He hath honour'd me of late, and I have bought
Golden opinions from all sorts of people,
Which would be worn now in their newest gloss,
Not cast aside so soon.

LADY MACBETH

Was the hope drunk,
Wherein you dress'd yourself? Hath it slept since?
And wakes it now to look so green, and pale,
At what it did so freely? From this time,
Such I account thy love. Art thou afeard
To be the same in thine own act, and valor,
As thou art in desire? Wouldst thou have that
Which thou esteem'st the ornament of life,
And live a coward in thine own esteem?
Letting I dare not, wait upon I would,
Like the poor cat i' th' adage?

MACBETH

Pr'ythee, peace:
I dare do all that may become a man,
Who dares do more is none.

LADY MACBETH

What beast was't then
That made you break this enterprise to me?
When you durst do it, then you were a man:
And to be more than what you were, you would
Be so much more the man. Nor time, nor place
Did then adhere, and yet you would make both:
They have made themselves, and that their fitness now
Does unmake you. I have given suck, and know
How tender 'tis to love the babe that milks me,
I would, while it was smiling in my face,
Have pluck'd my nipple from his boneless gums,
And dash'd the brains out, had I so sworn as you
Have done to this.

MACBETH

If we should fail?

LADY MACBETH

We fail?
But screw your courage to the sticking-place,
And we'll not fail: when Duncan is asleep,
(Whereto the rather shall his day's hard journey
Soundly invite him) his two chamberlains
Will I with wine, and wassail, so convince,
That memory, the warder of the brain,
Shall be a fume, and the receipt of reason
A limbec only: when in swinish sleep,
Their drenched natures lie as in a death,
What cannot you and I perform upon
The unguarded Duncan? What not put upon
His spongy officers? who shall bear the guilt
Of our great quell.

MACBETH
Bring forth men-children only:
For thy undaunted mettle should compose
Nothing but males. Will it not be receiv'd,
When we have mark'd with blood those sleepy two
Of his own chamber, and us'd their very daggers,
That they have don't?

LADY MACBETH
Who dares receive it other,
As we shall make our griefs and clamor roar,
Upon his death?

MACBETH
I am settled, and bend up
Each corporal agent to this terrible feat.
Away, and mock the time with fairest show,
False face must hide what the false heart doth know.
   (They exit. Drums.)

Act II

Scene i:

Inverness. Court within the Castle. Enter BANQUO and FLEANCE with a torch. Drums subside.

BANQUO
How goes the night, boy?

FLEANCE
The moon is down: I have not heard the clock.

BANQUO
And she goes down at twelve.

FLEANCE
I take't, 'tis later, sir.

BANQUO

Hold, take my sword:
There's husbandry in heaven,
Their candles are all out: take thee that too.
A heavy summons lies like lead upon me,
And yet I would not sleep:
Merciful powers, restrain in me the cursed thoughts
That nature gives way to in repose.

(Enter MACBETH, and SEYTON (WITCH 2 with a mask))

Give me my sword: who's there?

MACBETH

A friend.

BANQUO

What sir, not yet at rest? The king's a-bed.
He hath been in unusual pleasure,
And sent forth great largess to your offices.
This diamond he greets your wife withal,
By the name of most kind hostess,
And shut up in measureless content.

MACBETH

Being unprepar'd,
Our will became the servant to defect;
Which else should free have wrought.

BANQUO

All's well.
I dreamt last night of the three weird sisters:
To you they have show'd some truth.

MACBETH

I think not of them:
Yet when we can entreat an hour to serve,
We would spend it in some words upon that business,
If you would grant the time.

BANQUO
At your kind'st leisure.

MACBETH
If you shall cleave to my consent,
When 'tis, it shall make honor for you.

BANQUO
So I lose none,
In seeking to augment it, but still keep
My bosom franchis'd, and allegiance clear,
I shall be counsell'd.

MACBETH
Good repose the while.

BANQUO
Thanks sir: the like to you.
  (BANQUO and FLEANCE exit)

MACBETH
Go bid thy mistress, when my drink is ready,
She strike upon the bell. Get thee to bed.
  (Exit SEYTON. Enter WITCH 3, carrying a dagger. Though she is quite visible to the audience, she is invisible to MACBETH. She swirls the dagger through the air, dancing it toward and away from MACBETH through the course of the speech below. The other WITCHES creep in to watch unseen, hiding behind their bird's wing fans.)
Is this a dagger, which I see before me,
The handle toward my hand? Come, let me clutch thee:
I have thee not, and yet I see thee still.
Art thou not fatal vision, sensible
To feeling, as to sight? or art thou but
A dagger of the mind, a false creation,
Proceeding from the heat-oppressed brain?
I see thee yet, in form as palpable,
As this which now I draw.
  (MACBETH draws his dagger.)

Thou marshall'st me the way that I was going,
And such an instrument I was to use.
Mine eyes are made the fools o' the other senses,
Or else worth all the rest: I see thee still;
    (A red light comes up on WITCH 3 and her dagger.)
And on thy blade, and dudgeon, gouts of blood,
Which was not so before. There's no such thing:
    (Red light goes out. WITCH 3 sweeps away the dagger and crouches to watch MACBETH, still invisible to him.)
It is the bloody business, which informs
Thus to mine eyes. Now o'er the one half-world
Nature seems dead, and wicked dreams abuse
The curtain'd sleep: witchcraft celebrates
Pale Hecate's offerings: and wither'd murder,
Alarum'd by his sentinel, the wolf,
Whose howl's his watch, thus with his stealthy pace,
With Tarquin's ravishing strides, towards his design
Moves like a ghost. Thou sure and firm-set earth
Hear not my steps, which way they walk, for fear
Thy very stones prate of my whereabout,
And take the present horror from the time,
Which now suits with it. Whiles I threat, he lives:
Words to the heat of deeds too cold breath gives.
    (A bell rings.)
I go, and it is done: the bell invites me.
Hear it not, Duncan, for it is a knell,
That summons thee to heaven, or to hell.
    (Drums. MACBETH exits, dagger raised. All 3 WITCHES swirl across the stage and exit.)

Act II

Scene ii:

Enter LADY MACBETH. Drums subside.

                LADY MACBETH
That which hath made them drunk, hath made me bold:

What hath quench'd them, hath given me fire.
  (An owl shrieks.)
Hark, peace: it was the owl that shriek'd,
The fatal bell-man, which gives the stern'st good night.
He is about it, the doors are open
And the surfeited grooms do mock their charge
With snores. I have drugg'd their possets,
That death and nature do contend about them,
Whether they live, or die.

MACBETH
  (Off stage.)
Who's there? What ho?

LADY MACBETH
Alack. I am afraid they have awak'd,
And 'tis not done: th' attempt, and not the deed,
Confounds us: hark: I laid their daggers ready,
He could not miss 'em. Had he not resembled
My father as he slept, I had done't.
My husband?
  (Enter MACBETH in bloody clothes, carrying two bloody daggers.)

MACBETH
I have done the deed:
Didst thou not hear a noise?

LADY MACBETH
I heard the owl scream, and the crickets cry.
Did not you speak?

MACBETH
When?

LADY MACBETH
Now.

MACBETH
As I descended?

LADY MACBETH
Ay.

MACBETH
Hark, who lies i' the second chamber?

LADY MACBETH
Donalbain.

MACBETH
This is a sorry sight.
    (Looking at the bloody daggers in his hands.)

LADY MACBETH
A foolish thought, to say a sorry sight.

MACBETH
There's one did laugh in's sleep,
And one cried Murder, that they did wake each other:
I stood, and heard them: But they did say their prayers,
And address'd them again to sleep.

LADY MACBETH
There are two lodg'd together.

MACBETH
One cried God bless us, and Amen the other,
As they had seen me with these hangman's hands:
Listening their fear, I could not say Amen,
When they did say God bless us.

LADY MACBETH
Consider it not so deeply.

MACBETH
But wherefore could not I pronounce Amen?
I had most need of blessing, and Amen stuck in my throat.

Antigone & Macbeth

LADY MACBETH

These deeds must not be thought
After these ways: so, it will make us mad.

MACBETH

Me thought I heard a voice cry, Sleep no more:
Macbeth does murder sleep, the innocent sleep;
Sleep that knits up the ravell'd sleave of care,
The death of each day's life, sore labour's bath,
Balm of hurt minds, great nature's second course,
Chief nourisher in life's feast.

LADY MACBETH

What do you mean?

MACBETH

Still it cried, Sleep no more to all the house:
Glamis hath murder'd sleep, and therefore Cawdor
Shall sleep no more: Macbeth shall sleep no more.

LADY MACBETH

Who was it, that thus cried? why worthy thane,
You do unbend your noble strength, to think
So brainsickly of things: Go get some water,
And wash this filthy witness from your hand.
Why did you bring these daggers from the place?
They must lie there: go carry them, and smear
The sleepy grooms with blood.

MACBETH

I'll go no more:
I am afraid, to think what I have done:
Look on't again, I dare not.

LADY MACBETH

Infirm of purpose:
Give me the daggers:
   (She takes the daggers from him.)
the sleeping, and the dead,

Are but as pictures: 'tis the eye of childhood,
That fears a painted devil. If he do bleed,
I'll gild the faces of the grooms withal,
For it must seem their guilt.
   (She exits. Knocking from off stage.)

MACBETH

Whence is that knocking?
How is't with me, when every noise appals me?
What hands are here? hah: they pluck out mine eyes.
Will all great Neptune's ocean wash this blood
Clean from my hand? No: this my hand will rather
The multitudinous seas incarnadine,
Making the green one, red.
   (Re-enter LADY MACBETH, her hands bloody from her task.)

LADY MACBETH

My hands are of your color: but I shame
To wear a heart so white.
   (Knocking within.)
I hear knocking at the south entry:
Retire we to our chamber:
A little water clears us of this deed.
How easy is it then? your constancy
Hath left you unattended.
   (Knocking within.)
Hark, more knocking.
Get on your nightgown, lest occasion call us,
And show us to be watchers: be not lost
So poorly in your thoughts.

MACBETH

To know my deed,
   (Knocking within.)
'Twere best not know myself.
Wake Duncan with thy knocking:
I would thou couldst.
   (They exit.)

Act II

Scene iii:

Enter a PORTER. Knocking within.

PORTER
Here's a knocking indeed. If a man were porter of hell-gate, he should have old turning the key.
   (Knocking.)
Knock, knock, knock. Who's there, i' the name of Belzebub? Here's a farmer that hang'd
himself on the expectation of plenty: come in time; have napkins enow about you; here you'll sweat for't.
   (Knocking.)
Knock, knock. Who's there, in the other devil's name? Faith, here's an equivocator, that could swear in both the scales against either scale, who committed treason enough for God's sake, yet could not equivocate to heaven: O, come in, equivocator.
   (Knocking.)
Knock, knock, knock! Who's there? Faith, here's an English tailor come hither, for stealing out of a French hose: come in, tailor; here you may roast your goose.
   (Knocking.)
Knock, knock: never at quiet. But this place is too cold for hell. I'll devil-porter it no further: I had thought to have let in some of all professions, that go the primrose way to the everlasting bonfire.
   (Knocking.)
Anon, anon. I pray you, remember the porter.
   (Enter MACDUFF and LENNOX.)

MACDUFF
Was it so late, friend, ere you went to bed,
That you do lie so late?

PORTER
Faith sir, we were carousing till the second cock:
And drink, sir, is a great provoker of three things.

MACDUFF
What three things does drink especially provoke?

PORTER
Marry, sir, nose-painting, sleep, and urine. Lechery, sir, it provokes and unprovokes: it provokes the desire, but it takes away the performance. Therefore much drink may be said to be an equivocator with lechery: it makes him, and it mars him; it sets him on, and it takes him off; it persuades him, and disheartens him; makes him stand to, and not stand to: in conclusion, equivocates him in a sleep, and giving him the lie, leaves him.

MACDUFF
I believe, drink gave thee the lie last night.

PORTER
That it did, sir, i' the very throat on me; but I requited him for his lie, and (I think) being too strong for him, though he took up my legs sometime, yet I made a shift to cast him.

MACDUFF
Is thy master stirring?
Our knocking has awak'd him: here he comes.
   (Enter MACBETH, cleaned up and dressed for bed.)

LENNOX
Good morrow, noble sir.

MACBETH
Good morrow, both.

MACDUFF
Is the king stirring, worthy thane?

MACBETH
Not yet.

MACDUFF
He did command me to call timely on him,
I have almost slipp'd the hour.

MACBETH
I'll bring you to him.

MACDUFF
I know this is a joyful trouble to you:
But yet 'tis one.

MACBETH
The labour we delight in, physics pain:
This is the door.

MACDUFF
I'll make so bold to call, for 'tis my limited
service.
   (Exit MACDUFF.)

LENNOX
Goes the king hence to-day?

MACBETH
He does: he did appoint so.

LENNOX
The night has been unruly:
where we lay, our chimneys were blown down,
and (as they say) lamentings heard i' the air;
Strange screams of death,
And prophesying, with accents terrible,
Of dire combustion, and confus'd events,
New hatch'd to the woeful time.
The obscure bird clamour'd the live-long night.
Some say the earth was feverous,
And did shake.

MACBETH

'Twas a rough night.

LENNOX

My young remembrance cannot parallel
A fellow to it.
  (Re-enter MACDUFF.)

MACDUFF

O horror, horror, horror,
Tongue nor heart cannot conceive nor name thee.

MACBETH, LENNOX.

What's the matter?

MACDUFF

Confusion now hath made his masterpiece:
Most sacrilegious murder hath broke ope
The Lord's anointed temple, and stole thence
The life o' the building.

MACBETH

What is't you say, the life?

LENNOX

Mean you his majesty?

MACDUFF

Approach the chamber, and destroy your sight
With a new Gorgon. Do not bid me speak:
See, and then speak yourselves: awake, awake,
  (MACBETH and LENNOX exit.)
Ring the alarum bell: murder and treason,
Banquo, and Donalbain: Malcolm awake,
Shake off this downy sleep, and see
The great doom's image: Malcolm, Banquo,
As from your graves rise up,
To countenance this horror. Ring the bell.
  (Alarum-bell rings. Enter LADY MACBETH.)

LADY MACBETH

What's the business?
That such a hideous trumpet calls to parley
The sleepers of the house? speak, speak.

MACDUFF

O gentle lady,
'Tis not for you to hear what I can speak:
The repetition in a woman's ear,
Would murder as it fell.
    (Enter BANQUO, half-dressed.)
O Banquo, Banquo, Our royal master's murder'd.

LADY MACBETH

Woe, alas:
What, in our house?

BANQUO

Too cruel, any where.
Dear Duff, I pr'ythee, contradict thyself,
And say, it is not so.
    (Enter MACBETH and LENNOX, with ROSS.)

MACBETH

Had I but died an hour before this chance,
I had liv'd a blessed time: for from this instant,
There's nothing serious in mortality:
All is but toys: renown and grace is dead,
The wine of life is drawn, and the mere lees
Is left this vault, to brag of.
    (Enter MALCOLM and DONALBAIN.)

DONALBAIN

What is amiss?

MACBETH

You are, and do not know't:
The spring, the head, the fountain of your blood
Is stopp'd, the very source of it is stopp'd.

Absolute Macbeth

MACDUFF

Your royal father's murder'd.

MALCOLM

Oh, by whom?

LENNOX

Those of his chamber, as it seem'd, had done't:
Their hands and faces were all badg'd with blood,
So were their daggers, which unwip'd, we found
Upon their pillows: they star'd, and were distracted,
No man's life was to be trusted with them.

MACBETH

O, yet I do repent me of my fury,
That I did kill them.

MACDUFF

Wherefore did you so?

MACBETH

Who can be wise, amaz'd, temp'rate, and furious,
Loyal, and neutral, in a moment? No man:
Th' expedition of my violent love
Outrun the pauser, reason. Here lay Duncan,
His silver skin, lac'd with his golden blood,
And his gash'd stabs, look'd like a breach in nature,
For ruin's wasteful entrance: there the murderers,
Steep'd in the colours of their trade; their daggers
Unmannerly breech'd with gore: who could refrain,
That had a heart to love; and in that heart,
Courage, to make's love known?

LADY MACBETH

Help me hence, ho.
   (She faints.)

MACDUFF

Look to the lady.

(MACBETH, ROSS and others rush to aid LADY MAC-
BETH upstage. MALCOLM and DONALDBAIN move downstage, away from the others.)

MALCOLM

Why do we hold our tongues,
That most may claim this argument for ours?

DONALBAIN

What should be spoken here,
Where our fate hid in an auger hole,
May rush, and seize us? Let's away,
Our tears are not yet brew'd.

MALCOLM

Nor our strong sorrow
Upon the foot of motion.

BANQUO

Look to the lady:
And when we have our naked frailties hid,
That suffer in exposure; let us meet,
And question this most bloody piece of work,
To know it further. Fears and scruples shake us:
In the great hand of God I stand, and thence,
Against the undivulg'd pretense, I fight
Of treasonous malice.

MACDUFF

And so do I.

ALL

So all.

MACBETH

Let's briefly put on manly readiness,
And meet i' the hall together.

ALL

Well contented.
    (They all exit but MALCOLM and DONALBAIN.)

MALCOLM

What will you do?
Let's not consort with them:
To show an unfelt sorrow is an office
Which the false man does easy.
I'll to England.

DONALBAIN

To Ireland, I:
Our separated fortune shall keep us both the safer:
Where we are, there's daggers in men's smiles;
the near in blood, the nearer bloody.

MALCOLM

This murderous shaft that's shot,
Hath not yet lighted: and our safest way,
Is to avoid the aim. Therefore to horse,
And let us not be dainty of leave-taking,
But shift away: there's warrant in that theft,
Which steals itself, when there's no mercy left.
    (Drums. MALCOLM exits downstage right. DONALD-
BAIN exits upstage right and returns to the drums. The 3
WITCHES swirl across the scene and out.)

Act II

Scene iv:

The same. Without the Castle. Enter ROSS and an OLD
MAN. The drums subside.

OLD MAN

Threescore and ten I can remember well,
Within the volume of which time, I have seen

Hours dreadful, and things strange: but this sore night
Hath trifled former knowings.

ROSS

Ah, good father,
Thou seest the heavens, as troubled with man's act,
Threaten his bloody stage: by the clock 'tis day,
And yet dark night strangles the travelling lamp:
Is't night's predominance, or the day's shame,
That darkness does the face of earth entomb,
When living light should kiss it?

OLD MAN

'Tis unnatural,
Even like the deed that's done: On Tuesday last,
A falcon towering in her pride of place,
Was by a mousing owl hawk'd at, and kill'd.

ROSS

And Duncan's horses,
(a thing most strange, and certain)
Beauteous, and swift, the minions of their race,
Turn'd wild in nature, broke their stalls, flung out,
Contending 'gainst obedience, as they would
Make war with mankind.

OLD MAN

'Tis said, they eat each other.

ROSS

They did so:
To the amazement of mine eyes that look'd upon't.
Here comes the good Macduff.
    (Enter MACDUFF.)
How goes the world sir, now?

MACDUFF

Why see you not?

ROSS

Is't known who did this more than bloody deed?

MACDUFF

Those that Macbeth hath slain.

ROSS

Alas the day,
What good could they pretend?

MACDUFF

They were suborn'd,
Malcolm, and Donalbain the king's two sons
Are stol'n away and fled, which puts upon them
Suspicion of the deed.

ROSS

'Gainst nature still,
Thriftless ambition, that wilt raven up
Thine own life's means: Then 'tis most like,
The sovereignty will fall upon Macbeth.

MACDUFF

He is already nam'd, and gone to Scone
To be invested.

ROSS

Will you to Scone?

MACDUFF

No cousin, I'll to Fife.

ROSS

Well, I will thither.

MACDUFF

Well may you see things well done there: adieu.
Lest our old robes sit easier than our new.

Antigone & Macbeth

ROSS

Farewell, father.

OLD MAN

God's benison go with you; and with those
That would make good of bad, and friends of foes.
  (Drums. They exit.)

Act III

Scene i:

Forres. A Room in the Palace. Enter BANQUO. Drums subside.

BANQUO

Thou hast it now, king, Cawdor, Glamis, all,
As the weird women promis'd, and I fear
Thou play'dst most foully for't: yet it was said
It should not stand in thy posterity,
But that myself should be the root, and father
Of many kings. If there come truth from them,
As upon thee Macbeth, their speeches shine,
Why by the verities on thee made good,
May they not be my oracles as well,
And set me up in hope. But hush, no more.
  (Snare drum sounds. Enter MACBETH as king, LADY MACBETH as Queen; LENNOX, ROSS, SEYTON and two LORDS (WITCH 2, 1 & 3 carrying masks).)

MACBETH

Here's our chief guest.

LADY MACBETH

If he had been forgotten,
It had been as a gap in our great feast,
And all-thing unbecoming.

MACBETH

Tonight we hold a solemn supper sir,
And I'll request your presence.

BANQUO

Let your highness
Command upon me, to the which my duties
Are with a most indissoluble tie
For ever knit.

MACBETH

Ride you this afternoon?

BANQUO

Ay, my good lord.

MACBETH

We should have else desir'd your good advice
    (Which still hath been both grave, and prosperous)
In this day's council: but we'll take to-morrow.
Is't far you ride?

BANQUO

As far, my lord, as will fill up the time
'Twixt this, and supper. Go not my horse the better,
I must become a borrower of the night,
For a dark hour, or twain.

MACBETH

Fail not our feast.

BANQUO

My lord, I will not.

MACBETH

We hear our bloody cousins are bestow'd
In England, and in Ireland, not confessing
Their cruel parricide, filling their hearers
With strange invention. But of that tomorrow,

When therewithal, we shall have cause of state,
Craving us jointly. Hie you to horse:
Adieu, till you return at night.
Goes Fleance with you?

BANQUO

Ay, my good lord: our time does call upon's.

MACBETH

I wish your horses swift, and sure of foot:
And so I do commend you to their backs.
Farewell.
    (Exit BANQUO.)
Let every man be master of his time,
Till seven at night, to make society
The sweeter welcome:
We will keep ourself till supper time alone:
While then, God be with you.
    (All exit but SEYTON and MACBETH. WITCHES 1 & 3
use their bird's wing fans to make themselves invisible
and stay onstage to watch.)
Sirrah, a word with you: attend those men
Our pleasure?

SEYTON (WITCH 2)

They are, my lord, without the palace gate.

MACBETH

Bring them before us.
    (Exit SEYTON.)
To be thus is nothing, but to be safely thus
Our fears in Banquo stick deep,
And in his royalty of nature reigns that
Which would be fear'd. 'Tis much he dares,
And to that dauntless temper of his mind,
He hath a wisdom, that doth guide his valour,
To act in safety. There is none but he,
Whose being I do fear: and under him,
My genius is rebuk'd, as it is said

Absolute Macbeth

Mark Antony's was by Caesar. He chid the sisters,
When first they put the name of king upon me,
And bade them speak to him. Then prophet-like,
They hail'd him father to a line of kings.
Upon my head they plac'd a fruitless crown,
And put a barren sceptre in my gripe,
Thence to be wrench'd with an unlineal hand,
No son of mine succeeding: If't be so,
For Banquo's issue have I fil'd my mind,
For them, the gracious Duncan have I murder'd;
Put rancours in the vessel of my peace
Only for them, and mine eternal jewel
Given to the common enemy of man,
To make them kings, the seeds of Banquo kings.
Rather than so, come fate into the list,
And champion me to the utterance.
Who's there?
    (Re-enter SEYTON, with two MURDERERS.)
Now go to the door, and stay there till we call.
    (Exit SEYTON. WITCHES 1 & 3 (invisible) huddle close.)
Was it not yesterday we spoke together?

FIRST MURDERER

It was, so please your highness.

MACBETH

Well then,
Now have you consider'd of my speeches:
Know, that it was he, in the times past,
Which held you so under fortune,
Which you thought had been our innocent self.
This I made good to you, in our last conference,
Pass'd in probation with you:
How you were borne in hand, how cross'd:
The instruments: Who wrought with them:
And all things else, that might
To half a soul, and to a notion craz'd,
Say, Thus did Banquo.

FIRST MURDERER
You made it known to us.

MACBETH
I did so; and went further, which is now
Our point of second meeting.
Do you find your patience so predominant,
In your nature, that you can let this go?
Are you so gospell'd, To pray for this good man,
And for his issue, whose heavy hand
Hath bow'd you to the grave, and beggar'd
Yours forever?

FIRST MURDERER
We are men, my liege.

MACBETH
Ay, in the catalogue ye go for men,
As hounds, and greyhounds, mongrels, spaniels, curs,
Shoughs, water-rugs, and demi-wolves are clipt
All by the name of dogs: the valu'd file
Distinguishes the swift, the slow, the subtle,
The house-keeper, the hunter, every one
According to the gift, which bounteous nature
Hath in him clos'd; whereby he does receive
Particular addition, from the bill,
That writes them all alike: and so of men.
Now, if you have a station in the file,
Not i' the worst rank of manhood, say't,
And I will put that business in your bosoms,
Whose execution takes your enemy off,
Grapples you to the heart; and love of us,
Who wear our health but sickly in his life,
Which in his death were perfect.

SECOND MURDERER
I am one, my liege,
Whom the vile blows and buffets of the world
Have so incens'd that I am reckless what I do,
To spite the world.

Absolute Macbeth

FIRST MURDERER
And I another,
So weary with disasters, tugg'd with fortune,
That I would set my life on any chance,
To mend it, or be rid on't.

MACBETH
Both of you know Banquo was your enemy.

BOTH MURDERERS
True, my lord.

MACBETH
So is he mine: and in such bloody distance,
That every minute of his being, thrusts
Against my near'st of life: and though I could
With barefac'd power sweep him from my sight,
And bid my will avouch it; yet I must not,
For certain friends that are both his, and mine,
Whose loves I may not drop, but wail his fall,
Who I myself struck down: and thence it is,
That I to your assistance do make love,
Masking the business from the common eye,
For sundry weighty reasons.

SECOND MURDERER
We shall, my lord,
Perform what you command us.

FIRST MURDERER
Though our lives—-

MACBETH
Your spirits shine through you.
Within this hour, at most,
I will advise you where to plant yourselves;
Acquaint you with the perfect spy o' the time,
The moment on't, for't must be done tonight,
And something from the palace: always thought

That I require a clearness; and with him,
To leave no rubs nor botches in the work:
Fleance, his son, that keeps him company,
Whose absence is no less material to me,
Than is his father's, must embrace the fate
Of that dark hour: resolve yourselves apart,
I'll come to you anon.

BOTH MURDERERS
We are resolv'd, my lord.

MACBETH
I'll call upon you straight: abide within.
   (MURDERERS exit.)
It is concluded: Banquo, thy soul's flight,
If it find heaven, must find it out tonight.
   (Drums. MACBETH exits. WITCHES swirl around the space and exit.)

Act III

Scene ii:

The same. Another Room in the Palace. Enter LADY MACBETH and a SERVANT. Drums subside.

LADY MACBETH
Is Banquo gone from court?

SERVANT
Ay, madam, but returns again tonight.

LADY MACBETH
Say to the king, I would attend his leisure
For a few words.

SERVANT

Madam, I will.
   (Exit.)

LADY MACBETH

Naught's had, all's spent.
Where our desire is got without content:
'Tis safer to be that which we destroy,
Than by destruction dwell in doubtful joy.
   (Enter MACBETH.)
How now, my lord. Why do you keep alone?
Of sorriest fancies your companions making,
Using those thoughts, which should indeed have died
With them they think on: things without all remedy
Should be without regard: what's done is done.

MACBETH

We have scorch'd the snake, not kill'd it:
She'll close, and be herself, whilst our poor malice
Remains in danger of her former tooth.
But let the frame of things disjoint,
Both the worlds suffer,
Ere we will eat our meal in fear, and sleep
In the affliction of these terrible dreams,
That shake us nightly: Better be with the dead,
Whom we, to gain our peace, have sent to peace,
Than on the torture of the mind to lie
In restless ecstasy.
Duncan is in his grave:
After life's fitful fever, he sleeps well,
Treason has done his worst: nor steel, nor poison,
Malice domestic, foreign levy, nothing,
Can touch him further.

LADY MACBETH

Come on:
Gentle my lord, sleek o'er your rugged looks,
Be bright and jovial among your guests tonight.

MACBETH
O, full of scorpions is my mind, dear wife:
Thou know'st, that Banquo and his Fleance lives.

LADY MACBETH
What's to be done?

MACBETH
Be innocent of the knowledge, dearest chuck,
Till thou applaud the deed: Come, seeling night,
Scarf up the tender eye of pitiful day,
And with thy bloody and invisible hand
Cancel and tear to pieces that great bond,
Which keeps me pale. Light thickens,
Good things of day begin to droop and drowse,
Whiles night's black agents to their preys do rouse.
Thou marvell'st at my words: but hold thee still,
Things bad begun, make strong themselves by ill:
So, pr'ythee, go with me.
    (Drums. They exit.)

Act III

Scene iii:

A lane leading to the Palace. Enter three MURDERERS.
Drums subside.

FIRST MURDERER
But who did bid thee join with us?

THIRD MURDERER
Macbeth.

SECOND MURDERER
He needs not our mistrust; since he delivers
Our offices, and what we have to do,
To the direction just.

FIRST MURDERER
Then stand with us:
The west yet glimmers with some streaks of day.
Now spurs the lated traveller apace,
To gain the timely inn, and near approaches
The subject of our watch.

THIRD MURDERER
Hark. I hear horses.

BANQUO
(Within.)
Give us a light there, ho.

SECOND MURDERER
Then 'tis he:
The rest that are within the note of expectation,
Already are i' the court.

FIRST MURDERER
His horses go about.

THIRD MURDERER
Almost a mile: but he does usually,
So all men do, from hence to the palace gate
Make it their walk.

SECOND MURDERER
A light, a light.

THIRD MURDERER
'Tis he.

FIRST MURDERER
Stand to't.
(Enter BANQUO, and FLEANCE with a torch. BANQUO hands his fighting staff to FLEANCE and steps into the center to look at the sky.)

BANQUO
It will be rain tonight.

FIRST MURDERER
Let it come down.
    (He grabs FLEANCE from behind. SECOND MURDERER jumps on BANQUO's back as the THIRD MURDERER rushes in with his dagger.)

BANQUO
O, treachery.
    (They fight. BANQUO disarms one of the MURDERERS.)
Fly, good Fleance.
    (FLEANCE bites the FIRST MURDERER'S hand and stomps on his foot to escape him. BANQUO takes his first dagger wound helping FLEANCE escape.)
Fly, fly, fly. Thou mayst revenge.
    (FLEANCE escapes. All three MURDERER'S attack BANQUO with daggers, wearing him down with wounds.)
O slave.
    (BANQUO dies.)

THIRD MURDERER
Who did strike out the light?

FIRST MURDERER
Was't not the way?

THIRD MURDERER
There's but one down: the son is fled.

SECOND MURDERER
We have lost the best half of our affair.

FIRST MURDERER
Well, let's away, and say how much is done.

(They exit. The WITCHES swirl onto the stage, crying out with laments. Six veiled PALLBEARERS enter and carry away BANQUO'S body on their shoulders. The company sings the dirge *Kali Ma*. They exit in a stately march, singing. Curtain.)

INTERMISSION

ACT TWO

Act III

Scene iv:

The same. A Room of state in the Palace. A banquet prepared. Enter MACBETH, LADY MACBETH, ROSS, LENNOX, WITCHES (carrying masks as LORDS), and SERVANT (with wine).

MACBETH
You know your own degrees, sit down:
At first and last, the hearty welcome.

LORDS
Thanks to your majesty.
 (They take their places at the table, upstage right. They leave a seat mid table for MACBETH. LADY MACBETH sits at the head. The SERVANT pours wine for all, beginning with MACBETH.)

MACBETH
Ourself will mingle with society,
And play the humble host:
Our hostess keeps her state, but in best time
We will require her welcome.

LADY MACBETH
Pronounce it for me sir, to all our friends,
For my heart speaks, they are welcome.
    (Enter FIRST MURDERER, downstage left.)

MACBETH
See they encounter thee with their hearts' thanks
Both sides are even: here I'll sit i' the midst,
    (MACBETH indicates the seat mid table for himself. He notices the FIRST MURDERER, waiting in the shadows.)
Be large in mirth, anon we'll drink a measure
The table round.
    (MACBETH crosses down to the MURDERER.)
There's blood upon thy face.

FIRST MURDERER
'Tis Banquo's then.

MACBETH
'Tis better thee without, than he within.
Is he despatch'd?

FIRST MURDERER
My lord, his throat is cut, that I did for him.

MACBETH
Thou art the best o' the cut-throats,
Yet he's good that did the like for Fleance:
If thou didst it, thou art the nonpareil.

FIRST MURDERER
Most royal sir
Fleance is 'scap'd.

MACBETH
Then comes my fit again:
I had else been perfect;
Whole as the marble, founded as the rock;

As broad, and general, as the casing air:
But now I am cabin'd, cribb'd, confin'd, bound in
To saucy doubts, and fears. But Banquo's safe?

FIRST MURDERER

Ay, my good lord: safe in a ditch he bides,
With twenty trenched gashes on his head;
The least a death to nature.

MACBETH

Thanks for that:
There the grown serpent lies, the worm that's fled
Hath nature that in time will venom breed,
No teeth for the present. Get thee gone, to-morrow
We'll hear ourselves again.
  (Exit MURDERER.)

LADY MACBETH

My royal lord,
You do not give the cheer: the feast is sold
That is not often vouch'd, while 'tis a-making:
'Tis given, with welcome: to feed were best at home:
From thence, the sauce to meat is ceremony,
Meeting were bare without it.

MACBETH

Sweet remembrancer:
Now, good digestion wait on appetite,
And health on both.

LENNOX

May't please your highness sit.
  (Unseen by the others, the GHOST OF BANQUO
enters as the WITCHES gesture him in. He wears a veil
over him that makes him invisible to all. He sits in MAC-
BETH'S place.)

MACBETH

Here had we now our country's honor, roof'd,

Were the grac'd person of our Banquo present:
Who, may I rather challenge for unkindness,
Than pity for mischance.

ROSS

His absence, sir,
Lays blame upon his promise. Please't your highness
To grace us with your royal company?

MACBETH

The table's full.

LENNOX

Here is a place reserv'd sir.

MACBETH

Where?

LENNOX

(He gestures to the seat taken by BANQUO'S GHOST.)
Here my good lord.
(The WITCHES pull the veil off BANQUO'S GHOST. He is bloody from the wounds that killed him. He turns to face MACBETH.)
What is't that moves your highness?

MACBETH

(Recoiling in horror.)
Which of you have done this?

LORDS (WITCHES)

What, my good lord?

MACBETH

Thou canst not say I did it: never shake
Thy gory locks at me.

ROSS

Gentlemen rise, his highness is not well.

LADY MACBETH
Sit worthy friends: my lord is often thus,
And hath been from his youth. Pray you keep seat,
The fit is momentary, upon a thought
He will again be well. If much you note him
You shall offend him, and extend his passion,
Feed, and regard him not.
    (She crosses to MACBETH.)
Are you a man?

MACBETH
Ay, and a bold one, that dare look on that
Which might appal the devil.

LADY MACBETH
O proper stuff:
This is the very painting of your fear:
This is the air-drawn dagger which you said
Led you to Duncan. O, these flaws and starts
(Impostors to true fear) would well become
A woman's story, at a winter's fire
Authoriz'd by her grandmam: shame itself,
Why do you make such faces? When all's done
You look but on a stool.

MACBETH
Pr'ythee see there:
Behold, look, lo, how say you:
Why what care I, if thou canst nod, speak too.
If charnel houses, and our graves must send
Those that we bury, back; our monuments
Shall be the maws of kites.
    (The WITCHES put the veil back over BANQUO'S GHOST, making him invisible once more.)

LADY MACBETH
What? quite unmann'd in folly.

MACBETH
If I stand here, I saw him.

LADY MACBETH

Fie for shame.

MACBETH

Blood hath been shed ere now, i' the olden time
Ere humane statute purg'd the gentle weal:
Ay, and since too, murders have been perform'd
Too terrible for the ear. The times has been,
That when the brains were out, the man would die,
And there an end: but now they rise again
With twenty mortal murders on their crowns,
And push us from our stools. This is more strange
Than such a murder is.

LADY MACBETH

My worthy lord
Your noble friends do lack you.

MACBETH

I do forget:
Do not muse at me my most worthy friends,
I have a strange infirmity, which is nothing
To those that know me. Come, love and health to all,
Then I'll sit down: Give me some wine, fill full:
   (LADY MACBETH fills his goblet. He raises it.)
I drink to the general joy o' the whole table,
And to our dear friend Banquo, whom we miss:
Would he were here: to all, and him we thirst,
And all to all.

LORDS

   (All raise their goblets.)
Our duties, and the pledge.
   (They drink. The WITCHES take the veil back off BANQUO'S GHOST. MACBETH sees him and falls to the ground, dropping his wine goblet.)

MACBETH

Avaunt, and quit my sight, let the earth hide thee:

Thy bones are marrowless, thy blood is cold:
Thou hast no speculation in those eyes
Which thou dost glare with.

LADY MACBETH
(She rises, attempting to distract the others from MACBETH.)
Think of this, good peers
But as a thing of custom: 'tis no other,
Only it spoils the pleasure of the time.

MACBETH
(He struggles to his feet and pulls out his dagger as BANQUO'S GHOST approaches him. During the lines below, MACBETH retreats and slashes at the air as BANQUO'S GHOST hold out his hand to him.)
What man dare, I dare:
Approach thou like the rugged Russian bear,
The arm'd rhinoceros, or the Hyrcan tiger,
Take any shape but that, and my firm nerves
Shall never tremble. Or be alive again,
And dare me to the desert with thy sword:
(ROSS rises from his chair, alarmed.)
If trembling I inhabit then, protest me
The baby of a girl. Hence horrible shadow.
Unreal mockery hence.
(BANQUO'S GHOST pulls the veil back over his own head and exits.)
Why so, being gone
I am a man again:
(MACBETH notices ROSS standing.)
Pray you sit still.

LADY MACBETH
You have displaced the mirth,
Broke the good meeting, with most admir'd disorder.

MACBETH

(To LADY MACBETH)
Can such things be,
And overcome us like a summer's cloud,
Without our special wonder?
 (To ROSS, crossing to him.)
You make me strange
Even to the disposition that I owe,
When now I think you can behold such sights,
And keep the natural ruby of your cheeks,
When mine are blanch'd with fear.

ROSS

What sights, my lord?

LADY MACBETH

I pray you speak not: he grows worse and worse
Question enrages him: at once, good-night.
 (LORDS begin to line up to bid MACBETH a formal goodnight. LADY MACBETH, insistent:)
Stand not upon the order of your going,
But go at once.

LENNOX

Good-night, and better health
Attend his majesty.

LADY MACBETH

A kind good-night to all.
 (ROSS and LENNOX exit. The WITCHES use their fans to become invisible and remain onstage to watch.)

MACBETH

It will have blood they say:
Blood will have blood:
Stones have been known to move, and trees to speak:
Augurs, and understood relations, have
By magot-pies, and choughs, and rooks, brought forth
The secret'st man of blood. What is the night?

Antigone & Macbeth

LADY MACBETH
Almost at odds with morning, which is which.

MACBETH
How say'st thou, that Macduff denies his person
At our great bidding?

LADY MACBETH
Did you send to him sir?

MACBETH
I hear it by the way: but I will send:
There's not a one of them but in his house
I keep a servant fee'd. I will to-morrow,
(And betimes I will) to the weird sisters.
More shall they speak: for now I am bent to know
By the worst means, the worst, for mine own good,
All causes shall give way. I am in blood
Step't in so far that, should I wade no more,
Returning were as tedious as go o'er:
Strange things I have in head, that will to hand,
Which must be acted, ere they may be scann'd.

LADY MACBETH
You lack the season of all natures, sleep.

MACBETH
Come, we'll to sleep: My strange and self-abuse
Is the initiate fear, that wants hard use:
We are yet but young in deed.
  (Drums. They exit. The WITCHES swirl out after them.)

Act III

Scene vi:

  (Note: Act III Scene v of the original has been cut.)

Absolute Macbeth

Forres. A Room in the Palace. Enter LENNOX and CAITH-
NESS from upstage. They look about them to make sure
they are not overheard.

LENNOX

My former speeches,
Have but hit your thoughts
Which can interpret further: only I say
Thing's have been strangely borne. The gracious Duncan
Was pitied of Macbeth: marry he was dead:
And the right valiant Banquo walk'd too late,
Whom you may say, if't please you, Fleance kill'd,
For Fleance fled: Men must not walk too late.
Who cannot want the thought, how monstrous
It was for Malcolm, and for Donalbain
To kill their gracious father? damned fact.
How it did grieve Macbeth? did he not straight
In pious rage, the two delinquents tear,
That were the slaves of drink, and thralls of sleep?
Was not that nobly done?
    (SEYTON (WITCH 2) creeps on from upstage left to spy
on them.)
Ay, and wisely too:
For 'twould have anger'd any heart alive
To hear the men deny't. So that I say,
He has borne all things well, and I do think,
That had he Duncan's sons under his key,
(As, an't please heaven he shall not) they should find
What 'twere to kill a father: so should Fleance.
    (They notice SEYTON.)
But, peace;
    (They watch until SEYTON exits.)
for from broad words, and 'cause he fail'd
His presence at the tyrant's feast, I hear
Macduff lives in disgrace. Sir, can you tell
Where he bestows himself?

CAITHNESS

(He runs upstage to be assured SEYTON is gone, then rejoins LENNOX, center stage.)

The son of Duncan
    (From whom this tyrant holds the due of birth)
Lives in the English court, and is receiv'd
Of the most pious Edward, with such grace,
That the malevolence of fortune, nothing
Takes from his high respect. Thither Macduff
Is gone, to pray the holy king, upon his aid
To wake Northumberland, and warlike Siward,
That by the help of these (with Him above
To ratify the work) we may again
Give to our tables meat, sleep to our nights:
Free from our feasts, and banquets bloody knives:
Do faithful homage, and receive free honours,
All which we pine for now. And this report
Hath so exasperate the king, that he
Prepares for some attempt of war.

LENNOX

Sent he to Macduff?

CAITHNESS

He did: and with an absolute Sir, not I
The cloudy messenger turns me his back,
And hums; as who should say, You'll rue the time
That clogs me with this answer.

LENNOX

And that well might
Advise him to a caution, to hold what distance
His wisdom can provide. Some holy angel
Fly to the court of England, and unfold
His message ere he come, that a swift blessing
May soon return to this our suffering country
Under a hand accurs'd.

CAITHNESS
I'll send my prayers with him.
(Drums. They exit. The WITCHES rush in carrying the caldron and set it center stage.)

Act IV

Scene i:

A dark cave. In the middle, a caldron boiling. The drums continue. The WITCHES gather around the caldron to cast a spell. The drums play until the witches exit, sometimes dropping down to atmospheric sound effects to accompany the uncanny actions of the WITCHES.

FIRST WITCH
Thrice the brinded cat hath mew'd.

SECOND WITCH
Thrice, and once the hedge-pig whin'd.

THIRD WITCH
Harpier cries: tis time, 'tis time.

FIRST WITCH
(She kneels upstage of the caldron, opens her bag, and drops her ingredients into the caldron as she names them. The other two crouch downstage right and left of the caldron. They use their bird's wing fans to scoop some invisible spirits toward the caldron and to shoo others away.)
Round about the caldron go:
In the poison'd entrails throw
Toad, that under cold stone,
Days and nights has thirty-one:
Swelter'd venom sleeping got,
Boil thou first i' the charmed pot.

ALL
(They circle the caldron as they chant.)
Double, double, toil and trouble;
Fire burn, and caldron, bubble.

SECOND WITCH
(She kneels upstage of the caldron, opens her bag, and drops her ingredients into the caldron as she names them. The other two crouch downstage right and left of the caldron. They use their bird's wing fans, as before.)

Fillet of a fenny snake,
In the caldron boil and bake:
Eye of newt, and toe of frog,
Wool of bat, and tongue of dog:
Adder's fork, and blind-worm's sting,
Lizard's leg, and howlet's wing:
For a charm of powerful trouble,
Like a hell-broth, boil and bubble.

ALL
(They circle the caldron as they chant.)
Double, double, toil and trouble,
Fire burn, and caldron bubble.

THIRD WITCH
(She kneels upstage of the caldron. The other two crouch downstage right and left, as before.)
Scale of dragon, tooth of wolf,
Witch's mummy, maw and gulf
Of the ravin'd salt-sea shark:
Root of hemlock, digg'd i' the dark:
Liver of blaspheming fool,
Gall of goat, and slips of yew,
Finger of birth-strangl'd babe,
Ditch-deliver'd by a drab,
Make the gruel thick, and slab.
Add thereto a tiger's chaudron,
For the ingredients of our caldron.

Absolute Macbeth

ALL
(They circle the caldron.)
Double, double, toil and trouble,
Fire burn, and caldron bubble.
(The drums increase in intensity and the WITCHES dance throughout the space, completing the spell.)

FIRST WITCH
(Returning to the caldron to pour in the ingredient.)
Cool it with a baboon's blood,
Then the charm is firm and good.

SECOND WITCH
By the pricking of my thumbs,
Something wicked this way comes:
Open locks, whoever knocks.
(Enter MACBETH, upstage center.)

MACBETH
How now you secret, black, and midnight hags?
What is't you do?

ALL
A deed without a name.

MACBETH
I conjure you, by that which you profess,
(Howe'er you come to know it) answer me:
Though you untie the winds, and let them fight
Against the churches: though the yesty waves
Confound and swallow navigation up:
Though bladed corn be lodg'd, and trees blown down,
Though castles topple on their warders' heads:
Though palaces, and pyramids do slope
Their heads to their foundations: though the treasure
Of nature's germaine, tumble all together,
Even till destruction sicken: answer me
To what I ask you.

FIRST WITCH
Speak.

SECOND WITCH
Demand.

THIRD WITCH
We'll answer.

FIRST WITCH
Say, if thou'dst rather hear it from our mouths,
Or from our masters?

MACBETH
Call 'em: let me see 'em.
  (The WITCHES drag him swiftly to a kneeling position behind the caldron. They add more ingredients.)

FIRST WITCH
Pour in sow's blood, that hath eaten
Her nine farrow: grease that's sweaten
From the murderer's gibbet, throw
Into the flame.

ALL
Come high or low:
Thyself and office deftly show.
  (Special lights. Vigorous drumming. APPARITION ONE enters upstage carrying a veiled mask.)

MACBETH
Tell me, thou unknown power,

FIRST WITCH
He knows thy thought:
Hear his speech, but say thou naught.

APPARITION ONE
Macbeth, Macbeth, Macbeth: Beware Macduff, Beware the

Thane of Fife: Dismiss me: enough.
   (Exits.)

MACBETH

Whate'er thou art, for thy good caution, thanks
Thou hast harp'd my fear aright. But one word more.

FIRST WITCH

He will not be commanded: here's another
More potent than the first.
   (Lights. Drumming. APPARITION TWO enters upstage,
carrying a mask with a bloody veil.)

APPARITION TWO

Macbeth, Macbeth, Macbeth.

MACBETH

Had I three ears, I'd hear thee.

APPARITION TWO

Be bloody, bold, and resolute: Laugh to scorn the power
of man: for none of woman born shall harm Macbeth.
   (Exits.)

MACBETH

Then live, Macduff: what need I fear of thee?
But yet I'll make assurance double sure,
And take a bond of fate: thou shalt not live,
That I may tell pale-hearted fear, it lies;
And sleep in spite of thunder.
   (Lights. Drumming. APPARITION THREE enters
upstage, a Child carrying a veiled mask with a crown.)
What is this, that rises like the issue of a king,
And wears upon his baby brow, the round
And top of sovereignty?

ALL

Listen, but speak not to't.

APPARITION THREE

Be lion-mettled, proud, and take no care:
Who chafes, who frets, or where conspirers are:
Macbeth shall never vanquish'd be, until
Great Birnam wood, to high Dunsinane hill
Shall come against him.
   (Exits.)

MACBETH

That will never be:
Who can impress the forest, bid the tree
Unfix his earth-bound root? Sweet bodements, good:
Rebellious dead, rise never till the wood
Of Birnam rise, and our high-plac'd Macbeth
Shall live the lease of nature, pay his breath
To time, and mortal custom. Yet my heart
Throbs to know one thing: Tell me, if your art
Can tell so much: shall Banquo's issue ever
Reign in this kingdom?

ALL

Seek to know no more.

MACBETH

I will be satisfied. Deny me this,
And an eternal curse fall on you: Let me know.
Why sinks that caldron? and what noise is this?
   (Red lights on caldron. Drums.)

FIRST WITCH

Show.

SECOND WITCH

Show.

THIRD WITCH

Show.

Absolute Macbeth

ALL

Show his eyes, and grieve his heart,
Come like shadows, so depart.

(EIGHT KINGS wearing crowns and veils over their faces appear, and pass over in order, bloody BANQUO with a mirror in his hand following. (Note: we used four actors who circled the percussionists twice upstage to serve for the eight).)

MACBETH

Thou are too like the spirit of Banquo: down:
Thy crown does sear mine eyeballs. And thy hair
Thou other gold-bound brow, is like the first:
A third, is like the former. Filthy hags,
Why do you show me this? —— A fourth? Start, eyes!
What, will the line stretch out to the crack of doom?
Another yet? A seventh? I'll see no more:
And yet the eighth appears, who bears a glass,
Which shows me many more: and some I see
That twofold balls, and treble sceptres carry.
Horrible sight: Now I see 'tis true,
For the blood-bolter'd Banquo smiles upon me,
And points at them for his. What? is this so?

(The KINGS and BANQUO exit.)

FIRST WITCH

Ay sir, all this is so. But why
Stands Macbeth thus amazedly?
Come sisters, cheer we up his sprites,
And show the best of our delights.
I'll charm the air to give a sound,
While you perform your antic round:
That this great king may kindly say,
Our duties, did his welcome pay.

(Raucous drums. The WITCHES dance around MACBETH, terrifying him, and then exit abruptly. Drums subside.)

MACBETH
Where are they? Gone?
Let this pernicious hour,
Stand aye accursed in the calendar.
   (Shouting.)
Come in, without there.
   (Enter LENNOX.)

LENNOX
What's your grace's will?

MACBETH
Saw you the weird sisters?

LENNOX
No my lord.

MACBETH
Came they not by you?

LENNOX
No indeed my lord.

MACBETH
Infected be the air whereon they ride,
And damn'd all those that trust them. I did hear
The galloping of horse. Who was't came by?

LENNOX
'Tis two or three my lord, that bring you word:
Macduff is fled to England.

MACBETH
Fled to England?

LENNOX
Ay, my good lord.

MACBETH

Time, thou anticipat'st my dread exploits:
The flighty purpose never is o'ertook
Unless the deed go with it. From this moment,
The very firstlings of my heart shall be
The firstlings of my hand. And even now
To crown my thoughts with acts: be it thought and done:
The castle of Macduff, I will surprise.
Seize upon Fife; give to the edge o' the sword
His wife, his babes, and all unfortunate souls
That trace him in his line. No boasting like a fool,
This deed I'll do, before this purpose cool,
But no more sights. Where are these gentlemen?
Come, bring me where they are.
   (Drums. They exit.)

Act IV

Scene ii:

Fife. A Room in MACDUFF'S Castle. Enter LADY MAC-
DUFF, her SON, and ROSS. Drums subside.

LADY MACDUFF

What had he done, to make him fly the land?

ROSS

You must have patience madam.

LADY MACDUFF

He had none:
His flight was madness: when our actions do not,
Our fears do make us traitors.

ROSS

You know not
Whether it was his wisdom, or his fear.

LADY MACDUFF

Wisdom? to leave his wife, to leave his babes,
His mansion, and his titles, in a place
From whence himself does fly? He loves us not,
He wants the natural touch. For the poor wren,
(The most diminutive of birds) will fight,
Her young ones in her nest, against the owl:
All is the fear, and nothing is the love;
As little is the wisdom, where the flight
So runs against all reason.

ROSS

My dearest coz,
I pray you, school yourself. But, for your husband,
He is noble, wise, Judicious, and best knows
The fits o' the season. I dare not speak much further:
But cruel are the times, when we are traitors
And do not know ourselves; when we hold rumour
From what we fear, yet know not what we fear,
But float upon a wild and violent sea
Each way, and move. I take my leave of you:
Shall not be long but I'll be here again:
Things at the worst will cease, or else climb upward,
To what they were before. My pretty cousin,
Blessing upon you.

LADY MACDUFF

Father'd he is,
And yet he's fatherless.

ROSS

I am so much a fool, should I stay longer
It would be my disgrace, and your discomfort.
I take my leave at once.
    (ROSS exits.)

LADY MACDUFF

Sirrah, your father's dead;
And what will you do now? How will you live?

SON
As birds do mother.

LADY MACDUFF
What with worms, and flies?

SON
With what I get I mean, and so do they.

LADY MACDUFF
Poor bird,
Thou'dst never fear the net, nor lime,
The pit-fall, nor the gin.

SON
Why should I mother?
Poor birds they are not set for:
My father is not dead for all your saying.

LADY MACDUFF
Yes, he is dead:
How wilt thou do for father?

SON
Nay how will you do for a husband?

LADY MACDUFF
Why I can buy me twenty at any market.

SON
Then you'll buy 'em to sell again.

LADY MACDUFF
Thou speak'st with all thy wit,
And yet, i' faith with wit enough for thee.

SON
Was my father a traitor, mother?

LADY MACDUFF
Ay, that he was.

SON
What is a traitor?

LADY MACDUFF
Why one that swears, and lies.

SON
And be all traitors, that do so?

LADY MACDUFF
Everyone that does so, is a traitor, and must be hanged.

SON
And must they all be hanged, that swear and lie?

LADY MACDUFF
Every one.

SON
Who must hang them?

LADY MACDUFF
Why, the honest men.

SON
Then the liars and swearers are fools: for there are liars
and swearers enow, to beat the honest men,
And hang up them.

LADY MACDUFF
Now God help thee, poor monkey:
But how wilt thou do for a father?

SON
If he were dead, you'ld weep for him: if you
would not, it were a good sign that I should quickly
have a new father.

LADY MACDUFF
Poor prattler, how thou talk'st.
  (Enter a MESSENGER (WITCH 1, carrying a mask).)

MESSENGER (WITCH 1)
Bless you, fair dame: I am not to you known,
Though in your state of honor I am perfect;
I doubt some danger does approach you nearly.
If you will take a homely man's advice,
Be not found here: hence with your little ones.
To fright you thus, methinks, I am too savage;
To do worse to you were fell cruelty,
Which is too nigh your person. Heaven preserve you.
I dare abide no longer.
  (MESSENGER exits.)

LADY MACDUFF
Whither should I fly?
I have done no harm. But I remember now
I am in this earthly world: where to do harm
Is often laudable, to do good sometime
Accounted dangerous folly. Why then, alas,
Do I put up that womanly defense,
To say I have done no harm?
What are these faces?
  (Enter MURDERERS. Frightening atmospheric percussion begins, low.)

FIRST MURDERER
Where is your husband?

LADY MACDUFF
I hope in no place so unsanctified,
Where such as thou mayst find him.

SECOND MURDERER
He's a traitor.

SON
(Attacking the MURDERER with his toy.)
Thou liest, thou shag-haar'd villain.

SECOND MURDERER
(SECOND MURDERER grabs the SON. FIRST MURDERER grabs LADY MACDUFF, who struggles against him.)
What you egg?
(Stabbing him.)
Young fry of treachery?
(LADY MACDUFF screams.)

SON
He has kill'd me, mother,
Run away I pray you.
(SECOND MURDER drops SON to the ground. He dies. Louder drums. FIRST MURDERER forces LADY MACDUFF across the stage and against the wall. He holds her there, pulls out his dagger and stabs her. She cries out, slides down the wall and dies. The MURDERERS carry the bodies out on their shoulders. The WITCHES swirl through, crying a desperate lament.)

Act IV

Scene iii:

England. Before the King's Palace. Enter MALCOLM and MACDUFF. Drums subside.

MALCOLM
Let us seek out some desolate shade, and there
Weep our sad bosoms empty.

MACDUFF
Let us rather
Hold fast the mortal sword: and, like good men,

Absolute Macbeth

Bestride our down-fall'n birthdom: each new morn,
New widows howl, new orphans cry, new sorrows
Strike heaven on the face, that it resounds
As if it felt with Scotland, and yell'd out
Like syllable of dolour.

MALCOLM

What I believe, I'll wail;
What you have spoke, it may be so perchance.
This tyrant, whose sole name blisters our tongues,
Was once thought honest: you have loved him well,
He hath not touch'd you yet. I am young, but something
You may deserve of him through me.

MACDUFF

I am not treacherous.

MALCOLM

But Macbeth is.
A good and virtuous nature may recoil
In an imperial charge. But I shall crave your pardon:
That which you are, my thoughts cannot transpose;
Angels are bright still, though the brightest fell.
Though all things foul, would wear the brows of grace
Yet grace must still look so.

MACDUFF

I have lost my hopes.

MALCOLM

Perchance even there where I did find my doubts.
Why in that rawness left you wife, and child?
Those precious motives, those strong knots of love,
Without leave-taking. I pray you,
Let not my jealousies, be your dishonors,
But mine own safeties: you may be rightly just,
Whatever I shall think.

MACDUFF

Bleed, bleed poor country,
Great tyranny, lay thou thy basis sure,
For goodness dare not check thee: Fare thee well lord,
I would not be the villain that thou think'st,
For the whole space that's in the tyrant's grasp,
And the rich East to boot.

MALCOLM

Be not offended:
I speak not as in absolute fear of you:
I think our country sinks beneath the yoke,
It weeps, it bleeds, and each new day a gash
Is added to her wounds. I think withal,
There would be hands uplifted in my right:
And here from gracious England have I offer
Of goodly thousands. But for all this,
When I shall tread upon the tyrant's head,
Or wear it on my sword; yet my poor country
Shall have more vices than it had before,
More suffer, and more sundry ways than ever,
By him that shall succeed.

MACDUFF

What should he be?

MALCOLM

It is myself I mean: in whom I know
All the particulars of vice so grafted,
That when they shall be open'd, black Macbeth
Will seem as pure as snow.

MACDUFF

Not in the legions
Of horrid hell, can come a devil more damn'd
In evils, to top Macbeth.

MALCOLM

I grant him bloody, luxurious,

Absolute Macbeth

Sudden, malicious, and smacking of every sin
That has a name. But there's no bottom, none
In my voluptuousness: Your wives, your daughters,
Your matrons, and your maids, could not fill up
The cistern of my lust. Better Macbeth,
Than such an one to reign.

MACDUFF

Boundless intemperance
In nature is a tyranny; but fear not yet.
We have willing dames enough: there cannot be
That vulture in you, to devour so many
As will to greatness dedicate themselves.

MALCOLM

With this, there grows in my affection such
A stanchless avarice, that were I king,
I should cut off the nobles for their lands,
And my more-having, would be as a sauce
To make me hunger more.

MACDUFF

This avarice
Sticks deeper: grows with more pernicious root
Than summer-seeming lust; and it hath been
The sword of our slain kings: yet do not fear;
Scotland hath foysons, to fill up your will
Of your mere own. All these are portable,
With other graces weigh'd.

MALCOLM

But I have none. The king-becoming graces,
As justice, verity, temperance, stableness,
I have no relish of them. Nay, had I power, I should
Pour the sweet milk of concord into hell,
Uproar the universal peace, confound
All unity on earth.

MACDUFF
O Scotland, Scotland.

MALCOLM
If such a one be fit to govern, speak:
I am as I have spoken.

MACDUFF
Fit to govern.
No, not to live. O nation miserable!
With an untitled tyrant, bloody-scepter'd,
When shalt thou see thy wholesome days again?
Since that the truest issue of thy throne
By his own interdiction stands accurs'd
And does blaspheme his breed? Thy royal father
Was a most sainted king: the queen that bore thee,
Oftener upon her knees, than on her feet,
Died every day she lived. Fare-thee-well,
These evils thou repeat'st upon thyself,
Have banish'd me from Scotland. O my breast,
Thy hope ends here.

MALCOLM
Macduff, this noble passion
Child of integrity, hath from my soul
Wiped the black scruples, reconcil'd my thoughts
To thy good truth, and honour. Devilish Macbeth,
By many of these trains, hath sought to win me
Into his power: and modest wisdom plucks me
From over-credulous haste: but God above
Deal between thee and me; for even now
I put myself to thy direction, and
Unspeak mine own detraction. Here abjure
The taints, and blames I laid upon myself,
For strangers to my nature. I am yet
Unknown to woman, never was forsworn,
Scarcely have coveted what was mine own.
At no time broke my faith, and delight
No less in truth than life. My first false speaking

Was this upon myself. What I am truly
Is thine, and my poor country's to command:
Whither indeed, before thy here-approach
Old Siward with ten thousand warlike men
Already at a point, was setting forth:
Now we'll together, and the chance of goodness
Be like our warranted quarrel. Why are you silent?

MACDUFF

Such welcome, and unwelcome things at once
'Tis hard to reconcile.
    (Enter a DOCTOR.)

MALCOLM:

Well, more anon. Comes the king forth
I pray you?

ENGLISH DOCTOR

Ay sir: there are a crew of wretched souls
That stay his cure: their malady convinces
The great assay of art. But at his touch,
Such sanctity hath heaven given his hand,
They presently amend.

MALCOLM:

I thank you doctor.
    (Exit DOCTOR.)

MACDUFF:

What's the disease he means?

MALCOLM:

'Tis call'd the evil.
A most miraculous work in this good king,
Which often since my here remain in England,
I have seen him do: How he solicits heaven
Himself best knows: but strangely-visited people
All swoln and ulcerous, pitiful to the eye,
The mere despair of surgery, he cures,

Hanging a golden stamp about their necks,
Put on with holy prayers.

MACDUFF:
See, who comes here?
   (Enter ROSS.)
My ever-gentle cousin, welcome hither.

MALCOLM
Good God, betimes remove
The means that makes us strangers.

ROSS
Sir, amen.

MACDUFF
Stands Scotland where it did?

ROSS
Alas, poor country,
Almost afraid to know itself.

MACDUFF
How does my wife?

ROSS
Why well.

MALCOLM
What's the newest grief?

ROSS
When I came hither to transport the tidings
Which I have heavily borne, there ran a rumour
Of many worthy fellows that were out,
Which was to my belief witness'd the rather,
For that I saw the tyrant's power a-foot.
Now is the time of help; your eye in Scotland
Would create soldiers, make our women fight,
To doff their dire distresses.

MALCOLM

Be't their comfort
We are coming thither: gracious England hath
Lent us good Siward, and ten thousand men,
An older and a better soldier, none
That Christendom gives out.

ROSS

Would I could answer
This comfort with the like. But I have words
That would be howl'd out in the desert air,
Where hearing should not latch them.

MACDUFF

What concern they,
The general cause, or is it a fee-grief
Due to some single breast?

ROSS

No mind that's honest
But in it shares some woe, though the main part
Pertains to you alone.

MACDUFF

If it be mine
Keep it not from me, quickly let me have it.

ROSS

Let not your ears despise my tongue for ever,
Which shall possess them with the heaviest sound
That ever yet they heard.

MACDUFF

Humh. I guess at it.

ROSS

Your castle is surpris'd; your wife and babes
Savagely slaughter'd: to relate the manner
Were on the quarry of these murder'd deer
To add the death of you.

MALCOLM

Merciful heaven:
What man, ne'er pull your hat upon your brows:
Give sorrow words; the grief that does not speak,
Whispers the o'er-fraught heart, and bids it break.

MACDUFF

My children too?

ROSS

Wife, children, servants, all that could be found.

MACDUFF

And I must be from thence? My wife kill'd too?

ROSS

I have said.

MALCOLM

Be comforted.
Let's make us medicines of our great revenge,
To cure this deadly grief.

MACDUFF

He has no children. All my pretty ones?
Did you say all? O hell-kite! All?
What, all my pretty chickens, and their dam
At one fell swoop?

MALCOLM

Dispute it like a man.

MACDUFF

I shall do so:
But I must also feel it as a man;
I cannot but remember such things were
That were most precious to me: Did heaven look on,
And would not take their part? Sinful Macduff,
They were all struck for thee: Naught that I am,

Not for their own demerits, but for mine
Fell slaughter on their souls: heaven rest them now.

MALCOLM
Be this the whetstone of your sword, let grief
Convert to anger: blunt not the heart, enrage it.

MACDUFF
O, I could play the woman with mine eye,
And braggart with my tongue. But, gentle heavens,
Cut short all intermission: Front to front
Bring thou this fiend of Scotland and myself;
Within my sword's length set him, if he 'scape,
Heaven forgive him too.

MALCOLM
Come go we to the king, our power is ready,
Our lack is nothing but our leave. Macbeth
Is ripe for shaking, and the powers above
Put on their instruments: Receive what cheer you may,
The night is long that never finds the day.
   (Drums. They exit.)

Act V

Scene i:

Dunsinane. A Room in the Castle. Night. Enter a SCOTTISH DOCTOR and a WAITING-GENTLEWOMAN. Drums subside.

DOCTOR
I have two nights watched with you, but can perceive no truth in your report. When was it she last walked?

GENTLEWOMAN
Since his majesty went into the field, I have seen her rise from her bed, throw her nightgown upon her, unlock her

closet, take forth paper, fold it, write upon it, read it, afterwards seal it, and again return to bed; yet all this while in a most fast sleep.

DOCTOR
A great perturbation in nature, to receive at once the benefit of sleep, and do the effects of watching. In this slumbery agitation, besides her walking and other actual performances, what, at any time, have you heard her say?

GENTLEWOMAN
That sir, which I will not report after her.

DOCTOR
You may to me; and 'tis most meet you should.

GENTLEWOMAN
Neither to you nor any one; having no witness to confirm my speech. Lo you, here she comes.
   (Enter LADY MACBETH from upstage with a lit candle.)
This is her very guise; and upon my life fast asleep. Observe her; stand close.

DOCTOR
How came she by that light?

GENTLEWOMAN
Why, it stood by her: she has light by her continually; 'tis her command.

DOCTOR
You see her eyes are open.
   (LADY MACBETH sets down the candle and begins rubbing her hands together.)

GENTLEWOMAN
Ay, but their sense is shut.

DOCTOR
What is it she does now? Look how she rubs her hands.

GENTLEWOMAN
It is an accustomed action with her, to seem thus washing her hands: I have known her continue in this a quarter of an hour.

LADY MACBETH
Yet here's a spot.

DOCTOR
Hark, she speaks:
   (He takes out a notebook and a quill.)
I will set down what comes from her, to satisfy my remembrance the more strongly.

LADY MACBETH
Out damned spot: out I say. One; two; why then 'tis time to do't:
   (She rushes to the edge of the platform and stops, looking down.)
Hell is murky.
   (She lurches forward to address an imaginary Macbeth.)
Fie, my lord, fie, a soldier, and afeard? What need we fear who knows it, when none can call our power to account?
   (Sorowful. To the ground.)
Yet who would have thought the old man to have had so much blood in him.

DOCTOR
Do you mark that?

LADY MACBETH
The Thane of Fife, had a wife: where is she now? What, will these hands ne'er be clean? No more o' that my lord, no more o' that: you mar all with this starting.

DOCTOR
Go to, go to: you have known what you should not.

GENTLEWOMAN
She has spoke what she should not, I am sure of that: heaven knows what she has known.

LADY MACBETH
Here's the smell of the blood still: all the perfumes of Arabia will not sweeten this little hand. Oh, oh, oh.

DOCTOR
What a sigh is there? The heart is sorely charged.

GENTLEWOMAN
I would not have such a heart in my bosom, for the dignity of the whole body.

DOCTOR
Well, well, well,

GENTLEWOMAN
Pray God it be, sir.

DOCTOR
(He moves closer to get a better look at LADY MACBETH, who now seems calmed by despair.)
This disease is beyond my practice: yet I have known those which have walked in their sleep, who have died holily in their beds.

LADY MACBETH
(Turning suddenly to the DOCTOR and grabbing him.)
Wash your hands, put on your nightgown, look not so pale: I tell you yet again Banquo's buried; he cannot come out on's grave.
(She drops her hold of him.)

DOCTOR

Even so?

LADY MACBETH
(Moving upstage.)
To bed, to bed: there's knocking at the gate: come, come, come, come, give me your hand: what's done cannot be undone: to bed, to bed, to bed.
(She exits.)

DOCTOR

Will she go now to bed?

GENTLEWOMAN

Directly.

DOCTOR

Foul whisperings are abroad: unnatural deeds
Do breed unnatural troubles: infected minds
To their deaf pillows will discharge their secrets.
More needs she the divine, than the physician.
God, God, forgive us all. Look after her,
Remove from her the means of all annoyance,
And still keep eyes upon her: so, good-night,
My mind she has mated, and amaz'd my sight.
I think, but dare not speak.

GENTLEWOMAN

Good-night good doctor.
(Drums. The GENTLEWOMAN retrieves LADY MACBETH'S candle. They exit.)

Act V

Scene ii:

English Forces march across stage to drums.

Act V

Scene iii:

Dunsinane. A Room in the Castle. Enter MACBETH in a manic state and the DOCTOR.

MACBETH
Bring me no more reports; let them fly all:
Till Birnam wood remove to Dunsinane,
I cannot taint with fear. What's the boy Malcolm?
Was he not born of woman? The spirits that know
All mortal consequences, have pronounc'd me thus:
Fear not Macbeth, no man that's born of woman
Shall e'er have power upon thee. Then fly false thanes,
And mingle with the English epicures,
The mind I sway by, and the heart I bear,
Shall never sag with doubt nor shake with fear.
    (Enter a MESSENGER (WITCH 1, carrying fright mask).)
The devil damn thee black, thou cream-fac'd loon:
Where gott'st thou that goose look?

MESSENGER (WITCH 1)
There is ten thousand

MACBETH
Geese villain?

MESSENGER (WITCH 1)
Soldiers sir.

MACBETH
Go prick thy face, and over-red thy fear
Thou lily-liver'd boy. What soldiers, patch?
Death of thy soul, those linen cheeks of thine
Are counsellors to fear. What soldiers whey-face?

MESSENGER (WITCH 1)
The English force, so please you.

MACBETH
Take thy face hence.
    (Exit MESSENGER. MACBETH calls out.)
Seyton,
    (To DOCTOR.)
I am sick at heart, When I behold:
    (MACBETH calls out.)
Seyton, I say,
    (Aside.)
This push will chair me ever, or disseat me now.
I have liv'd long enough: my way of life
Is fall'n into the sear, the yellow leaf;
And that which should accompany old age,
As honour, love, obedience, troops of friends,
I must not look to have: but in their stead,
Curses, not loud but deep, mouth-honour, breath
Which the poor heart would fain deny, and dare not.
    (MACBETH calls out.)
Seyton?
    (Enter SEYTON (WITCH 2).)

SEYTON (WITCH 2)
What's your gracious pleasure?

MACBETH
What news more?

SEYTON (WITCH 2)
All is confirm'd my lord, which was reported.

MACBETH
I'll fight, till from my bones, my flesh be hack'd.
Give me my armour.

SEYTON (WITCH 2)
'Tis not needed yet.

MACBETH

I'll put it on:
Send out more horses, skirr the country round,
Hang those that talk of fear. Give me mine armour:
   (SEYTON exits.)
How does your patient, doctor?

DOCTOR

Not so sick my lord,
As she is troubled with thick-coming fancies
That keep her from her rest.

MACBETH

Cure her of that:
Canst thou not minister to a mind diseas'd,
Pluck from the memory a rooted sorrow,
Raze out the written troubles of the brain,
And with some sweet oblivious antidote
Cleanse the stuff'd bosom, of that perilous stuff
Which weighs upon the heart?

DOCTOR

Therein the patient
Must minister to himself.
   (SEYTON returns with the armour.)

MACBETH

Throw physic to the dogs, I'll none of it.
Come, put mine armour on;
   (DOCTOR attempts to help him put on his armour.)
give me my staff: Seyton, send out:
   (SEYTON hands MACBETH his staff and exits.)
Doctor, the Thanes fly from me:
Come sir, despatch. If thou couldst doctor, cast
The water of my land, find her disease,
And purge it to a sound and pristine health,
I would applaud thee to the very echo,
That should applaud again.
   (MACBETH loses patience with the DOCTOR'S

attempts to put on his armour.)
Pull't off I say,
    (The DOCTOR pulls the armour off MACBETH.)
What rhubarb, senna, or what purgative drug
Would scour these English hence: Hear'st ye of them?

DOCTOR

Ay my good lord; your royal preparation
Makes us hear something.

MACBETH

Bring it after me:
I will not be afraid of death and bane,
Till Birnam forest come to Dunsinane.
    (MACBETH exits.)

DOCTOR

Were I from Dunsinane away, and clear,
Profit again should hardly draw me here.
    (Drums. He exits, carrying the armour after MACBETH.)

Act V

Scene iv:

Country near Dunsinane. Enter MALCOLM, OLD SIWARD and his SON, MACDUFF, LENNOX, ROSS, and FLEANCE, dressed for battle. Drums subside.

MALCOLM

Cousins, I hope the days are near at hand
That chambers will be safe.

LENNOX

We doubt it nothing.

SIWARD

What wood is this before us?

LENNOX

The wood of Birnam.

MALCOLM

Let every soldier hew him down a bough,
And bear't before him, thereby shall we shadow
The numbers of our host, and make discovery
Err in report of us.

LENNOX & ROSS

It shall be done.

SIWARD

We learn no other, but the confident tyrant
Keeps still in Dunsinane, and will endure
Our setting down before't.

MALCOLM

'Tis his main hope:
For where there is advantage to be given,
Both more and less have given him the revolt;
And none serve with him, but constrained things,
Whose hearts are absent too.

MACDUFF

Let our just censures
Attend the true event, and put we on
Industrious soldiership.
   (They all cheer.)

SIWARD

The time approaches,
That will with due decision make us know
What we shall say we have, and what we owe:
Thoughts speculative, their unsure hopes relate,
But certain issue, strokes must arbitrate,
Towards which advance the war.
   (They cheer again. Drums. They exit.)

Absolute Macbeth

Act V

Scene v:

Dunsinane. Within the castle. Enter MACBETH, SEYTON (WITCH 2), and TWO SOLDIERS. Drums subside.

MACBETH
Hang out our banners on the outward walls,
    (SOLDIER 1 exits to obey.)
The cry is still, they come: our castle's strength
Will laugh a siege to scorn: Here let them lie,
Till famine and the ague eat them up:
Were they not forc'd with those that should be ours,
We might have met them dareful, beard to beard,
And beat them backward home.
    (A cry of women within.)
What is that noise?

SEYTON (WITCH 2)
It is the cry of women, my good lord.
    (SEYTON and SOLDIER 2 exit to investigate.)

MACBETH
I have almost forgot the taste of fears:
The time has been, my senses would have cool'd
To hear a night-shriek, and my fell of hair
Would at a dismal treatise rouse, and stir
As life were in't. I have supp'd full with horrors,
Direness familiar to my slaught'rous thoughts
Cannot once start me.
    (Re-enter SEYTON (WITCH 2).)
Wherefore was that cry?

SEYTON (WITCH 2)
The queen, my lord, is dead.

MACBETH
She should have died hereafter;

There would have been a time for such a word:
To-morrow, and to-morrow, and to-morrow,
Creeps in this petty pace from day to day,
To the last syllable of recorded time:
And all our yesterdays, have lighted fools
The way to dusty death. Out, out, brief candle,
Life's but a walking shadow, a poor player,
That struts and frets his hour upon the stage,
And then is heard no more. It is a tale
Told by an idiot, full of sound and fury
Signifying nothing.
   (Enter a MESSENGER (WITCH 1, fright mask).)
Thou com'st to use thy tongue: thy story quickly.

MESSENGER (WITCH 1)
Gracious my lord,
I should report that which I say I saw,
But know not how to do it.

MACBETH
Well, say sir.

MESSENGER (WITCH 1)
As I did stand my watch upon the hill
I look'd toward Birnam, and anon methought,
The wood began to move.

MACBETH
Liar, and slave.
   (Striking him.)

MESSENGER (WITCH 1)
Let me endure your wrath, if't be not so:
Within this three mile may you see it coming.
I say, a moving grove.

MACBETH
If thou speak'st false,
Upon the next tree shalt thou hang alive,

Till famine cling thee: if thy speech be sooth,
I care not if thou dost for me as much.
I pull in resolution, and begin
To doubt the equivocation of the fiend,
That lies like truth. Fear not, till Birnam wood
Do come to Dunsinane, and now a wood
Comes toward Dunsinane. Arm, arm, and out,
If this which he avouches, does appear,
There is nor flying hence, nor tarrying here.
I 'gin to be a-weary of the sun,
And wish the estate o' the world were now undone.
Ring the alarum bell, blow wind, come wrack,
At least we'll die with harness on our back.
　　(Drums. They exit.)

Act V

Scene vi:

A plain before the castle. Enter MALCOLM. He shouts off-stage to the others.

MALCOLM

Now near enough:
Your leafy screens throw down,
And show like those you are:
　　(Enter OLD SIWARD and his SON, MACDUFF,
LENNOX, ROSS, and FLEANCE. To OLD SIWARD.)
You, worthy uncle,
Shall with my cousin your right-noble son
Lead our first battle. Worthy Macduff, and we
Shall take upon's what else remains to do,
According to our order.

SIWARD

Fare you well.
Do we but find the tyrant's power tonight,
Let us be beaten, if we cannot fight.
　　(They cheer.)

MACDUFF
Make all our trumpets speak, give them all breath
Those clamorous harbingers of blood, and death.
(They cheer. Drums. They exit. YOUNG SIWARD remains.)

Act V

Scene vii:

The same. Another part of the Plain. Enter MACBETH. Drums subside.

MACBETH
They have tied me to a stake, I cannot fly,
But bear-like I must fight the course. What's he
That was not born of woman? Such a one
Am I to fear, or none.
(YOUNG SIWARD slaps his weapons together. MACBETH sees him for the first time.)

YOUNG SIWARD
What is thy name?

MACBETH
Thou'lt be afraid to hear it.

YOUNG SIWARD
No: though thou call'st thyself a hotter name
Than any is in hell.

MACBETH
My name's Macbeth.

YOUNG SIWARD
The devil himself could not pronounce a title
More hateful to mine ear.

MACBETH

No: nor more fearful.

YOUNG SIWARD

Thou liest abhorred tyrant, with my sword
I'll prove the lie thou speak'st.
 (They fight, and YOUNG SIWARD is slain.)

MACBETH

Thou wast born of woman;
But swords I smile at, weapons laugh to scorn,
Brandish'd by man that's of a woman born.
 (MACBETH exits. Drums. Enter MACDUFF. Drums subside.)

MACDUFF

That way the noise is: Tyrant show thy face,
If thou be'st slain, and with no stroke of mine,
My wife and children's ghosts will haunt me still:
I cannot strike at wretched kerns, whose arms
Are hired to bear their staves; either thou Macbeth,
Or else my sword with an unbatter'd edge
I sheathe again undeeded. There thou shouldst be,
By this great clatter, one of greatest note
Seems bruited. Let me find him Fortune,
And more I beg not.
 (MACDUFF exits. Drums. Enter MALCOLM and OLD SIWARD. Drums subside.)

SIWARD

This way my lord, the castle's gently render'd:
The tyrant's people, on both sides do fight,
The noble thanes do bravely in the war,
The day almost itself professes yours,
And little is to do.

MALCOLM

We have met with foes
That strike beside us.

SIWARD

Enter sir, the castle.
   (They exit. Drums.)

Act V

Scene viii:

The same. Another part of the field. Enter MACBETH. Drums subside.

MACBETH

Why should I play the Roman fool, and die
On mine own sword? whiles I see lives, the gashes
Do better upon them.
   (MACBETH begins to exit. Enter MACDUFF.)

MACDUFF

Turn hell-hound, turn.

MACBETH

Of all men else I have avoided thee:
But get thee back, my soul is too much charg'd
With blood of thine already.

MACDUFF

I have no words,
My voice is in my sword, thou bloodier villain
Than terms can give thee out.
   (They fight.)

MACBETH

Thou losest labour:
As easy mayst thou the intrenchant air
With thy keen sword impress, as make me bleed:
Let fall thy blade on vulnerable crests,
I bear a charmed life, which must not yield
To one of woman born.

Absolute Macbeth

MACDUFF

Despair thy charm,
And let the angel whom thou still hast serv'd
Tell thee, Macduff was from his mother's womb
Untimely ripp'd.

(The WITCHES rush onto the scene, repeating the phrase "Untimely ripp'd." They crouch to watch, unseen by the others.)

MACBETH

Accursed be that tongue that tells me so;
For it hath cow'd my better part of man:
And be these juggling fiends no more believ'd,
That palter with us in a double sense,
That keep the word of promise to our ear,
And break it to our hope. I'll not fight with thee.

MACDUFF

Then yield thee coward,
And live to be the show, and gaze o' the time.
We'll have thee, as our rarer monsters are
Painted upon a pole, and underwrit,
Here may you see the tyrant.

MACBETH

I will not yield
To kiss the ground before young Malcolm's feet,
And to be baited with the rabble's curse.
Though Birnam wood be come to Dunsinane,
And thou oppos'd, being of no woman born,
Yet I will try the last. Lay on Macduff,
And damn'd be him, that first cries Hold, enough.

(They fight and MACBETH is slain. The WITCHES circle around his body.)

WITCHES

Now 'tis now, the tyrant's dead;
Now 'tis now, shall lose his head.
Thus we ask please free this world;

From in our midst his evil hurl.
And all around, this cure shall spread;
Remove from us that which we dread.

(Six veiled PALLBEARERS enter and lift MACBETH onto their shoulders. The company sings a more festive version of the dirge, *Kali Ma*. They carry MACBETH'S body off-stage, singing.)

(Enter MALCOLM, OLD SIWARD, ROSS, LENNOX, and FLEANCE.)

MALCOLM
I would the friends we miss, were safe arriv'd.

SIWARD
Some must go off: and yet by these I see,
So great a day as this is cheaply bought.

MALCOLM
Macduff is missing, and your noble son.

ROSS
Your son my lord, has paid a soldier's debt,
He only liv'd but till he was a man,
The which no sooner had his prowess confirm'd
In the unshrinking station where he fought,
But like a man he died.

SIWARD
Then he is dead?

FLEANCE
Ay, and brought off the field: your cause of sorrow
Must not be measur'd by his worth, for then
It hath no end.

SIWARD
Had he his hurts before?

ROSS
Ay, on the front.

SIWARD

Why then, God's soldier be he.
Had I as many sons, as I have hairs,
I would not wish them to a fairer death:
And so his knell is knoll'd.

MALCOLM

He's worth more sorrow,
And that I'll spend for him.

SIWARD

He's worth no more,
They say he parted well, and paid his score,
And so God be with him. Here comes newer comfort.
   (Re-enter MACDUFF carrying MACBETH'S bloody
head in a sack.)

MACDUFF

Hail king, for so thou art.
behold, where stands
The usurper's cursed head: the time is free:
   (They cheer.)
I see thee compass'd with thy kingdom's pearl,
That speak my salutation in their minds:
Whose voices I desire aloud with mine.
Hail King of Scotland.

ALL

Hail King of Scotland.

MALCOLM

We shall not spend a large expense of time,
Before we reckon with your several loves,
And make us even with you. My thanes and kinsmen
Henceforth be earls, the first that ever Scotland
In such an honour nam'd: What's more to do,
Which would be planted newly with the time,
As calling home our exil'd friends abroad,
That fled the snares of watchful tyranny,

Producing forth the cruel ministers
Of this dead butcher, and his fiend-like queen;
Who (as 'tis thought) by self and violent hands,
Took off her life. This, and what needful else
That calls upon us, by the grace of Grace,
We will perform in measure, time, and place:
So thanks to all at once, and to each one,
Whom we invite to see us crown'd at Scone.
    (Drums. They exit.)

CURTAIN

Polarity Ensemble Theatre: The First Season

Our first season has been an extraordinary journey. We selected the stories of two tyrants, each battling for his deepest desire and ending in destruction. However, the intrinsic style of these plays is different. Shakespeare intricately and subtly weaves the webs of deceit. There is no subtlety in the way the characters of a Greek tragedy charge toward destruction.

Our mission for Polarity is to bring a new edge to the classics and to produce new works. We seek to bring theatre back to its origins where the passions of the actors are the focus. We want our audience to take away inspired ideas that touch them emotionally and stir them to thought and conversation and change. And while the two plays are similar in theme, the approach and the productions were very different.

Let me begin with *Absolute Macbeth*: a play that brutally displays the power of evil and the consequences for anyone who seeks it. There is a famous curse on *Macbeth* that has actors calling it "The Scottish Play" in fear of bad luck at the mention of its name. Director Richard Engling did not believe the bad luck arose from saying *Macbeth* but from pronouncing the spells in the script itself. To purge the curse, he turned the power of evil back on itself by adding moments of ritual and additional text that focused the power of the enchantments.

When studying *Macbeth* in college, the focus was always on the complexities of the characters and their choices. What I found in our production was that the operation of temptation and evil is more simple than I thought. It comes down to one idea: you call upon evil and it will come. The consequence of bringing deceit into your life is often greater than you imagine. In the case of Macbeth and his Lady, the consequence is extreme. By using elements of ritual to protect the actors and audience, that energy could be sent out as a healing power into the world. The audience experienced the descent into violence, madness and death and participated in the ritual of purgation. They were involved emotionally and viscerally, bringing a new experience to a Shakespearean classic.

While *Absolute Macbeth* was about the consequences of inviting evil into the realm, *Antigone* is about justice versus rigidity in times of crisis. The tragedy of *Antigone* is that none of the characters pause to examine whether their past decisions still carry merit. They don't realize that the circumstances surrounding their initial decisions may have changed. If a leader does not question whether his actions are just, he can become a tyrant. A mistake can turn fatal. Justice becomes a weapon leaving unnecessary victims.

The audiences in Greek plays were meant to have enough emotional distance to see the mistakes of the characters and to know how to avoid making the same. Unlike *Absolute Macbeth*, the audience does not participate in the ritual, but the didactic experience makes them more conscious of avoiding the pitfalls of pride and prejudice. The audience leaves *Antigone* talking about whether the tragedy could have been avoided and how it applies to our world today.

Adaptations for a War-Torn Time

Antigone and *Absolute Macbeth* are two plays that depict different sides of a complex issue—a perfect selection for Polarity Ensemble Theatre's inaugural season. We hope you've enjoyed them.

—Ann Keen, Managing Director
Polarity Ensemble Theatre

Thanks to Our Patrons

On the occasion of this, our first published book, we would like to thank all our Founding Patrons whose generosity has allowed us to produce our first two shows and to launch our publishing efforts.

Gaia and Chronos Founding Patrons ($1,000+)
Anonymous (2)
Eric Cherry
Terry and Laurie Christiansen
Lois J. Hobart
The Weinberg Family Foundation

Aphrodite and Dionysos Founding Patrons ($500+)
The Geoffroy Family
Jody Miller and Rich Horvitz
Dean Matthews
Jack and Linda Richeson

Athena and Apollo Founding Patrons ($100+)
Michelle Adelman
Susan Arenberg
Maureen and Joseph Bardusk
CPR, Inc.
Irene and Charles Custer

Liz Davidson and Charley Custer
Maureen and Christopher Dillon
James Engling
Emily Erickson
Nancy Kauper
Roy and Cathy Keller
G. and G. Konigsfeld
Steven Kozak
Lynn Hyndman and Lee Mixon
Pat Monaghan
The J.P. Morgan Chase Foundation
Patrice and Bob Prescott
Mark and Angela Randall
Christy Sahler
George Solomon
Jim Tifft
Gregg Vogel
Cecilia Lynch and Tom Warnke
George and Romaine Wilcinski
Troy P. Young
Scott and Nancy Zordan

Founding Patrons ($40+)
Dori Fujii and Otis Berry
Pam and Peter Butterfield
Tim Carollo
John and Ann Cirpinski
Gloria Bond Clunie
Ann and Russ Covode
Greg Daniels
Georgann Charuhas and Randy Didderrich
Carl Fitzpatrick
Dan Frick
Sandy Greenberg
Erika and Dave Hamilton
Sue Dean and Jeff Jacobs
Jack and Judie Keen
Joseph Kilikevice
Brian Krusienski

Jennifer Krupinski
Sandra Mims
Felicia and John Przekota
Free Polazzo
Kay Rubsam
Mary Jane Seger
Gerry Shavitz
Lloyd Shields
Bridget Sullivan
Gerry Shavitz
Sharon Solwitz and Barry Silesky
Joanna Spilioti
Bob and Eric Thomassie
Steve and Leslie Warner
Jonathan and Lisa Weis
Julie E. Kaufman and Beth Wright
Simon Dixon and Janelle Zauha

Friends (Up to $40)
Violet Altmeyer
Donald Austin
Maria DiMonte
Carolyn Greenwood
Cheryl and Rich Kenney
Anna Marie Mullaney
Deborah Pausz
Outrider Press
Constance Schoen
Chris and John Seger
Duncan Storlie
Tallgrass Writers Guild
Chuck Wemstrom

The Polarity Ensemble Theatre is a registered Illinois Not-for-Profit Corporation and has Federal 501(c)(3) status as a public charity. Donations are tax-deductible to the full extent allowable by law.

www.ingramcontent.com/pod-product-compliance
Lightning Source LLC
Chambersburg PA
CBHW031247290426
44109CB00012B/468